GONE FOR A SOLDIER

A HISTORY OF LIFE IN THE BRITISH RANKS FROM 1642

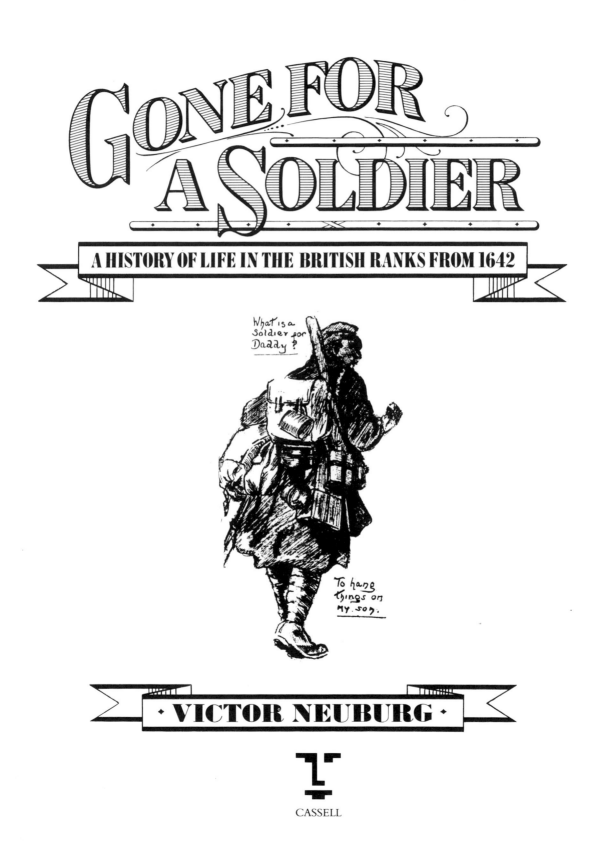

What is a soldier for Daddy?

To hang things on MY son.

VICTOR NEUBURG

CASSELL

For Anne, again

First published 1989 by Cassell Publishers Ltd,
Artillery House, Artillery Row, London SW1P 1RT

An Albion Book

Conceived, designed and produced by The Albion Press Ltd,
P.O. Box 52, Princes Risborough, Aylesbury, Bucks HP17 9PR

Text copyright © Victor E. Neuburg 1989
Volume copyright © The Albion Press Ltd 1989

British Library Cataloguing in Publication Data
Neuburg, Victor E.
Gone for a soldier: a history of life in the British ranks from 1642
1. Great Britain – Army – Soldiers – Army Life, 1642-1988
I. Title
355.1′0941
ISBN 0 304 32243 1

Designer: Emma Bradford
Editor: Robyn Marsack

Typesetting and origination by York House Typographic, London
Printed and bound in Great Britain by Oxford University Press

CONTENTS

Arouse *Britons* for the Honour and Glory of *Old England!*

Now is the Moment my noble-minded Countrymen, now is the Crisis of our Country's Fate!

Fly to the Standard of our Sovereign, hasten to man his Fleets and augment his Armies.

By acting thus, *Britons*, you shall restore the native Resplendency of our Beloved Country, chastise the Perfidious *French* and *Spaniards*, and be again united to our Brethren in *America*, who have been so basely deluded from their Natural Allegiance by the sworn Enemies of *All Englishmen*.

ALL REAL
VOLUNTEERS

Whose Hearts are filled with Loyalty for the best of Kings, and Love for the Noblest of Constitutions, and who are willing to maintain the Honour of OLD ENGLAND in Defiance of FRENCH and SPANISH Treachery, have now a noble Opportunity of obtaining immortal Renown, by repairing to the Standard of

His Majesty's 88th Regiment of Foot,
OR
BRITISH VOLUNTEERS,
COMMANDED BY
Colonel THOMAS KEATING,
Now quartered in *Sheffield*, in *Yorkshire*.

The Sons of Freedom are alone worthy to support the Honour of OLD ENGLAND, and the Conduct of the Noble Regiment of BRITISH VOLUNTEERS, shall prove that ENGLISHMEN never wanted Courage to defend their Wives, their Sweethearts, or their Firesides.

Such Gentlemen as chuse to serve their King and Country in the above-mentioned Regiment are desired to repair to the Drum-Head, or to

where they shall receive as large a Bounty as is given by any Regiment in his Majesty's Service (besides oth   Advantages) enter into immediate Pay and free Quarters, and be treated with every Attention that can be hoped for by a g   DIER.

GOD save

N. B. Bringers of Recruits may depend on being most liberally rewarded.

Printed by C. FOURDRINIER, Stationer, Charing-Cross.

INTRODUCTION

The British Army is a curious institution which has survived general apathy, much parliamentary prejudice and the parsimony of an almost always reluctant Treasury. There has been, too, an anti-army ideology which found its most outspoken expression in the seventeenth century. An anonymous pamphlet issued in 1697 argued that 'a Standing Army is inconsistent with a Free Government, and absolutely destructive to the Constitution of the English Monarchy.' This point of view, or something pretty close to it, was current for many years, and still finds adherents today.

With two exceptions, from 1916 to 1919 and from 1939 to 1963 when there was conscription, service in the British Army has always been on a voluntary basis. Compulsion to serve has traditionally been regarded with suspicion, and even with downright hostility. A regular force did not come into being until 1660, in the long and ambiguous shadow cast by Oliver Cromwell's New Model Army; and for nearly thirty years after its inception this new regular force was held by some to be constitutionally illegal. As G.M. Trevelyan said: 'It is no easy matter to reconcile the institution of a standing army with the genius of parliamentary and popular government, and the work was not done in a day' (*England Under Queen Anne*, Vol. I). Even today, in the closing decades of the twentieth century, it is interesting to ponder the fact that there is a Royal Navy and a Royal Air Force . . . but not a Royal Army.

The rather chequered history of the army reflects, I believe, a love-hate relationship of extremely long standing between civilians and soldiers. Led almost invariably bravely, even though too often indifferently, the army has played a crucial part in our history, and it is a history which has been dominated by war and conflict rather than by the orderly progress of parliamentary organisation and economic institutions for which liberal, Whig historians have – often elegantly, though ultimately inconclusively – long argued. Their view, in which war is seen as an aberration disturbing an essentially peaceful process, seems to me to fly in the face of facts, and to diminish the importance of the army in the history of Great Britain.

Every institution is dependent, in both its creation and its running, upon human beings. Thus military institutions depend upon soldiers, and it is the purpose of this book to tell something of their lives over some three centuries. In writing it I am concerned mainly with the experiences of non-commissioned officers and men ('other ranks', in the army's immortal phrase), and there are two reasons for this emphasis. First, memoirs of generals and other officers – almost always articulate, and often entertaining – abound. Secondly, too much military history has been written in terms of strategy, tactics and the biographies of those who ran successful campaigns and won battles. More often than not it is through the eyes of

OPPOSITE:
This recruiting poster belongs to the period of the American Revolution. The 88th Foot was raised under an order dated 19 October 1779, and disbanded in 1783 at the cessation of hostilities. In 1793 the regiment was reformed as The Connaught Rangers and was disbanded in 1922, on the establishment of the Irish Free State.

officers that we see army life – officers who were influential in their own times and present high and attractive profiles to posterity; but such an angle of vision is, to say the least, misleading. We should remember that in numerical terms 'other ranks' have always constituted a majority in the army, and if we are to have a balanced view of soldiers and their lives it is equally valuable to look at their experiences. Their testimony is less easy to track down. Many of those who served in the ranks were inarticulate, or for various reasons reluctant to put pen to paper, but when their voices can be heard amongst the clamorous priorities of history they are without fail worth listening to. Indeed, army life cannot be understood, except in the most superficial way, without them.

Oddly enough perhaps, it was Dr Samuel Johnson in the eighteenth century who anticipated this view. He contended in his forthright essay 'On the Bravery of the English Common Soldier' that men were motivated 'neither by possessions nor by notions of liberty'. Bravery, he argued, sprang from the Englishman's 'want of subordination', and 'they who complain in peace, of the insolence of the populace, must remember, that their insolence in peace is bravery in war.' Whatever might be said of Johnson's view, it seems apparent that, like Milton in an earlier century, he saw insolence as a human and even individual characteristic. For Johnson, the common soldier was a person and not just a cog in the military machine.

*   *   *

What we do not sufficiently realise about army life, I believe, is that so little of it is spent in actual fighting. We need all the help we can get if we are to arrive at even the most elementary sense of that life, and of military experience vis-à-vis officers and their men. Fortunately, it is arguable that soldiers as human beings do not change very much over time, despite the undoubted changes in the technologies of war which govern their lives. An infantry sergeant who fought at Malplaquet would have had much in common with his opposite number who fought his way to Thiepval rather more than two centuries later . . . even if the same cannot be said about their respective commanders, Marlborough and Haig. A small episode will serve as a focus for the soldier's life over the period we are looking at.

The struggle for Thiepval took place during the summer of 1916 when the British Expeditionary Force on the Western Front, with some support from the French Army, was engaged in the Battle of the Somme. In reality this was a series of bitterly fought engagements lasting several months and centred upon villages and hamlets laid waste by repeated heavy shelling: there were Mametz, Fricourt, Beaumont Hamel and Flers; there were Delville Wood, High Wood, and disputed areas of ground to which the BEF gave names like Sausage Valley, Caterpillar Wood, Needle Dump and Rose Trench. Today, more than seventy years later, the immensity of human suffering on both sides continues to beggar the imagination. BEF casualties alone were something like 60,000 on the first day of the battle, and the many military cemeteries in this area (the British ones beautifully

A dismounted cavalryman of the Cromwellian period. His small amount of body armour is similar to that worn today by the Household Cavalry on ceremonial occasions. The projection on his helmet is to protect his face from sword cuts.

Religious service *c.* 1800. The army, except in Cromwellian days, was never much interested in doctrine and saw religion in rather more pragmatic terms: collective acts of worship were valued as a contribution to morale and good order, especially church parades, for which men had to spend much time making themselves look spick and span. The Army Chaplain's Department, consisting of Anglican priests only, was formed in 1796. In 1827 Presbyterian ministers were authorized; Roman Catholics in 1836; Wesleyans in 1881, and the first Jewish chaplain was appointed in 1892. Army chaplains did not wear uniform until 1860.

tended by the Commonwealth War Graves Commission) still bear moving, silent witness to the human cost of war.

One man present at the battle was Private Edge of the 2nd Battalion Royal Welch Fusiliers. A regular soldier, described by his sergeant-major as 'a bit on the weak side', Edge had landed in France in August 1914 and gone through the retreat from Mons without becoming a straggler. He had subsequently carried out all his duties as a combatant soldier, and then the Medical Officer had made him a member of the unit canteen staff. In army parlance this was a 'cushy number', with few parades and a fairly comfortable billet in the rear when the battalion was in the front line. In August 1916 the 2nd Royal Welch Fusiliers were involved in heavy fighting at High Wood. It was a distinctly unhealthy place, with much of the area around the wood within range of enemy artillery fire. One morning at the height of the battle Private Edge – 'Sunny Jim', as he was known to his contemporaries – turned up in the trenches, without equipment or rifle but with a large pack slung over his shoulder. He had a slight speech defect, and in response to a curt enquiry as to what he wanted Edge replied: 'I fort the boys would want some cigawettes, so I've bwought some up.' He was allowed to go round the companies in the line until his stock was exhausted; then he plodded back to the rear. All in all it was a round trip of fourteen miles over poor roads and tracks, and for much of it he would have been under enemy fire. He made the trip, unbidden, to bring some form of comfort to his comrades. (See J.C. Dunn, *The War the Infantry Knew*, 1938; 1987.)

There is no obvious moral to this story – a very tiny episode in a prolonged and bloody enterprise – but it does tell us something about one soldier. Similar memories are all too rare. There was an anonymous Private of the 71st Regiment (later 1st Battalion Highland Light Infantry) who wrote in his autobiography, *Journal of a Soldier of the Seventy-First Regiment . . . from 1800 to 1815* published in 1822, that the morning after the Battle of Vittoria in 1813 he had awoken 'dull, stiff and weary' with his shoulder 'black as coal', the result of bruising from the recoil of his musket from which he had fired 108 rounds during the fighting. Then, too, there was a soldier of the 58th Regiment (later 2nd Battalion Northamptonshire Regiment), Samuel Ancell, whose *Circumstantial Journal of the . . . Siege of Gibraltar. In a Series of Letters . . .* was

These antics in a British camp in the Crimea in 1856 show soldiers dressed in blackface as a troop of 'Ethiopian' serenaders, with improvised instruments comprising an imitation banjo, a concertina, a tin whistle, a tin dish as tambourine and, of course, 'the bones'. The men are mimicking one of the most popular entertainments of the London streets at this date.

published in Liverpool in 1785. He wrote to his brother in England about the high cost of unrationed provisions during what he described as the 'long and tedious blockade and siege of Gibraltar' from 1779 to 1783. A goose, for example, cost £1.30 – a very high price in those days.

With few such exceptions, the other ranks of the army have remained at best faceless, a crowd of men in uniform who have rarely escaped some degree of condescension from posterity; and at worst they were seen as a danger to society, when not actually fighting its battles or manning its imperial outposts. 'We serve no redcoats here', said Kipling's publican, and the soldier outside his licensed premises was left to reflect upon the 'thin red line of 'eroes when the drums begin to roll . . .'. Throughout the period covered by this book, and even earlier, the publican's attitude was a common one. For many working-class families, 'going for a soldier' was regarded as the last resort, and even in the 1920s and beyond, considerable prejudice survived against enlisting in the army.

Nevertheless, there have always been men who actively sought a military career in the ranks or, if forced into it, then made a success of being a soldier. They became sergeants, quartermaster-sergeants and sergeants-major, earning money and enjoying a standard of living and a status which they were unlikely to achieve as labourers, tradesmen or clerks. Such men were often highly regarded. 'The choice of a Sergeant-major', wrote Bennett Cuthbertson in his *System for the Compleat Interior Management and Oeconomy of a Battalion of Infantry* (Dublin, 1768), 'must never be influenced by any consideration, than that of real merit . . .' Sergeants, he went on, should demonstrate 'honesty, sobriety, and a remarkable attention to every part of duty, with a neatness in their dress, and a quickness of understanding above the common run of Soldiers.' This theme was echoed some one hundred years later in the *Standing Orders* of the King's Own Regiment, published in 1857. 'A high sense of honour and respectability is indispensable to his situation', wrote the anonymous author describing the qualities to be found in a Sergeant-Major.

We know, for example, of three men who had such qualities. Thomas Borrow (George Borrow, author of *Lavengro* and other books, was his son) enlisted in 1783, became a sergeant nine years later and eventually rose to the rank of captain. Roger Lamb served in America during the Revolution, and his lively *Memoir of His Own Life* (Dublin, 1811) formed the basis of two novels by Robert Graves, *Sergeant Lamb of the Ninth* and *Proceed Sergeant Lamb*. Finally there was William Cobbett, who made the leap from Corporal to Sergeant-Major, as he wrote, over the heads of thirty sergeants who were senior to him. What minimised their anger and affront at such promotion was, Cobbett tells us, his habit of early rising. In summer he rose at daylight, and in winter at four. 'Long before any other man was dressed for parade, my work for the morning was well done . . .'; and he paraded the battalion just as 'the bayonets glistened in the rising sun . . . ' (*The Progress of a Plough-Boy to a Seat in Parliament*, ed. William Reitzel, 1933). Men like Borrow, Lamb and Cobbett formed the backbone of the army, and were instrumental in its day-to-day running.

Rifleman of the North York Militia (Light Infantry Regiment), 1814. Their bottle-green uniforms are similar to those worn by The Rifle Brigade, raised in 1800 as the Experimental Corps of Riflemen. These 'light' troops were trained to skirmish and to engage the enemy by making use of natural cover rather than by standing in line and firing their muskets in controlled volleys, as the 'heavy' infantry did at this period.

11

The command post of the 2nd Battalion Scots Guards on Goat Ridge during the Falklands campaign.

As senior non-commissioned officers, and together with the corporals and privates from whose ranks they had been promoted, they made up the largest number of serving soldiers at every period of the army's history. Their story has to a great extent gone by default, but it is worth the telling.

A tough strand of continuity runs through their story. The men named above were the descendants of Cromwell's Corporals of Horse, and among their successors were the sergeants and warrant officers who endured the heat of India and Africa; who were defeated in America (not because their courage faltered, but because the task facing the army was impossible); who froze at Sebastopol; who stormed the Ancre Heights; who were to be found on every front in the Second World War. Wherever the army has been deployed they have been prominent in the life of individual units – and today there are women amongst their number. It is safe to assume that without them the plans of politicians and generals would have come to nothing. For the historian they provide the most satisfactory focus for a study of life as other ranks have experienced it: and it can, I believe, be concluded that the gallantry of soldiers has always been bought too cheaply by successive governments, and that for the soldiers themselves comfortable footwear and adequate provisions have always been regarded as more important than the qualities of their senior officers or the rhetoric of politicians.

Chapter 1

RECRUITING

Finding enough volunteers to fill the ranks of the army has always been a problem. Even today, when techniques of advertising and selection are extremely sophisticated, the problem has not been entirely solved. In the past it was tackled at a personal level: the army went to look for men, and the sound of a drum in the square or market place of a provincial town gave reality to the phrase 'beating up for recruits'. It was an endless process, permitted everywhere except in the City of London. Small parties, usually consisting of a captain, a sergeant, a drummer and two private soldiers detached from their regiment, scoured the country for recruits. If volunteers were not readily forthcoming, or when especially large numbers of men were required, the government of the day could, and often did, have recourse to impressment.

In theory, voluntary enlistment remained the primary method of getting soldiers, and recruiting parties were warned 'not to use any Villanies or low practices to trapan recruits'; but it does seem unlikely that silver-tongued non-commissioned officers like Sergeant Kite did not upon occasion mislead them. It was not unknown for men to 'inlist' for a shilling without claiming the bounty to which, as we shall see, volunteers were entitled. Sergeant Kite, in fact, is the earliest recruiting sergeant of whom we have any knowledge. He is a major character in George Farquhar's play *The Recruiting Officer*, first produced at the Theatre Royal, Drury Lane, in April 1706. The author had been commissioned as a Lieutenant of Grenadiers in 1704, and was assigned to recruiting duties in the midland counties of England. After a period in Lichfield he moved to Shrewsbury, where the play is set and was, reputedly, written. There is some reason to believe that several of the leading characters are based upon local people, and that Kite is modelled upon a Sergeant Jones who was Farquhar's assistant in the recruiting party. Whatever the truth of this, there seems no doubt at all that Kite is portrayed as a real 'old soldier' – one who, like 'Old Bill' or 'The Good Soldier Švejk', knew all the tricks of his trade. As the play opens he is addressing a crowd in the market place:

> If any gentlemen soldiers, or others, have a mind to serve Her Majesty, and pull down the French King; if any prentices have severe masters, any children have undutiful parents; if any servants have too little wages, or any husband too much wife; let them repair to the noble Sergeant Kite, at the Sign of the Raven, in this good town of Shrewsbury, and they shall receive present relief and entertainment. – Gentlemen, I don't beat my drums here to ensnare or inveigle any man; for you must know, gentlemen, that I am a man of honour. Besides, I don't beat up for common soldiers; no, I list only grenadiers, grenadiers, gentlemen.

Beating up for recruits in 1781. The procedure was traditional and resembles that employed by Sergeant Kite in Farquhar's *The Recruiting Sergeant*. Here the sergeant is tempting the rustics with the promise of ready money. In practice, men joining up often received less than was promised. Complexities of the pay system and questionable methods employed by recruiters meant that new soldiers might have little cash in hand after they had been charged for necessaries.

Men were persuaded by the blandishments and promises of recruiters like Kite. Some enlisted because they were attracted by a military career: others were quite simply duped. Criminals might join to avoid arrest – the army was a fairly safe haven from the law; debtors seeking to avoid imprisonment, malcontents, vagabonds, unemployed apprentices and journeymen might be amongst recruits. The precise identity of men who served in the ranks of the seventeenth- and eighteenth-century army cannot be determined. It is worth mentioning, though, that financial penalties could be imposed upon the recruiting officer who enlisted unsuitable men.

Once a man was enlisted and had 'taken the shilling' he was entitled to receive a bounty. The practice of paying levy money amounting to £1 had begun in 1678 to stimulate voluntary enlistment, but since it was paid directly by the Treasury to the captain who commanded the recruit's troop or company, it was up to this officer to strike the best bargain he could with the newly joined soldier. It seems to have been not uncommon for the bounty to be five or ten shillings. By the middle of the eighteenth century the enlistment sum was larger, but one pound of this was withheld to pay for 'necessaries', and it would have been extremely unwise for any soldier, however strong-minded, to stand upon his undoubted legal right to the entire sum. Had he done so and arrived at his regiment 'bare of necessaries', he would have been put under immediate stoppages of pay at the rate of six pence per day in order to pay for them. Some regiments, it is worth noting, did seek to attract recruits by offering a higher bounty.

During the Civil War recruiting for the army could be easier when men were willing to serve on a local basis and when squires and landowners could exert pressure upon their tenants and workforce to join regiments which they were raising for the Royalist or the Parliamentary side. All the same, there were difficulties in finding men for service and impressment became increasingly common. A pressed man was, in theory, a less satisfactory soldier than a volunteer – he was more likely to be disgruntled, and harsh discipline could not make him more than an unwilling soldier. In practice this was not entirely true, for voluntary service could attract 'bad bargains' to the colours whereas impressment might just bring some good men into the ranks. In 1651, for example, Parliament ordered 10,000 men to be raised to reinforce the army in Ireland. It was said at the time that the pressed men were of better quality than the volunteers! Some years later, in 1659, eight sergeants from Colonel Monck's Regiment of Foot (later the Coldstream Guards) were sent from Scotland into England on recruiting duty, and they had instructions to re-enlist such old soldiers as they could find, and to take care that such men behaved well on the march or be responsible for any misbehaviour. It is not known how many veterans were forthcoming.

By the end of the seventeenth century recruiting had become a never-ending concern for the army. For regiments stationed in England it went on all year round, while units stationed in Flanders sent home recruiting parties during the winter months to raise men for the new campaigning season which began each spring. It was easier to find men for the cavalry and the dragoons than for the infantry: pay was better, and horsemen enjoyed a higher social status. Procedures were fairly standard. Recruiting parties would lodge in an ale house in a town or large village and then begin to beat up for men. Once a few had been gathered, they would be escorted to Regimental Headquarters if the unit was stationed in England or to a port of embarkation if it was serving overseas. Hanging about, or

A recruiting party of the 33rd Foot at work in the early nineteenth century. Public houses like this one were obvious places for finding new men, and for generating the bonhomie that went with enlistment. They also provided accessible lodgings for recruiting parties.

waiting for a ship, could be a tedious business, and such enforced leisure provided for some, as we shall see, an opportunity to desert with a few shillings in hand – and even to desert and re-enlist in another regiment in order to claim another bounty payment.

Sometimes dubious tactics were employed to lure men into the army, and the acceptance of money proffered by an officer or soldier for whatever reason carried with it the risk of being enlisted. George Venables was sitting in the George Inn at Hatfield, Hertfordshire, one evening in the last years of the seventeenth century when a soldier named John White came in. The two struck up a conversation, and during the course of it White showed Venables a shilling coin, saying that there was something strange about it. The latter was unwise enough to take it in his hand and examine it; and when he went to return it, White told him that he had enlisted and would not take back the coin. In this instance Venables refused to be tricked and threw the coin to the floor. (See John Childs, *The British Army of William III*, 1987.) Another device was for the recruiter to pretend that a man was a deserter, so that pressing him into the service would look to any bystander like the arrest of an offender.

From 1 March 1693 it became a legal requirement for every recruit to be taken before a Justice of the Peace to 'declare his free consent to be listed or mustered as a soldier', but such a safeguard against illegal practices was not always effective. In 1694 it came to the notice of the House of Commons that Michael Tooley, Provost-Marshal of the Coldstream Guards, was running a highly profitable, though quite irregular, business of supplying recruits. He had a house in Holborn where about two hundred men were held. They had been either lured there upon some pretext or another, or kidnapped in the street. Once in the house they were in effect prisoners, and were regarded as fair game. There was no question of attestation before a J.P.; the men were sold at a profit to officers who wanted them, and compelled to serve in the ranks. Other Provost-Marshals ran similar profitable undertakings and neither Parliament nor the army was disposed to interfere. As to why so glaring an infringement of a recent law went unquestioned in the capital city, one can only suppose that many believed the military authorities to be performing a useful public service by taking riff-raff, vagabonds and homeless men off the streets and providing them with clothes, food and pay – to say nothing of the opportunity to work for society! In the case of Tooley, eventually the London mob intervened and his house was seriously damaged in a riot (see Childs, pp.111–12).

Methods of raising men at this time, then, comprised legal means, kidnapping, impressment, and even offering to convicted criminals the chance to join up as an alternative to punishment. This last method had the advantage of being cheap and convenient. In Scotland in 1691 the Privy Council ordered magistrates to deliver 'burdensome and expensive' prisoners to Colonel George Ramsey, who commanded the Scottish troops being sent to Flanders. Two years later it was not uncommon for men convicted of fairly minor offences at the Old Bailey in London to be sentenced to obligatory enlistment. In Kenilworth, Warwickshire, a

Recruiting at a fair-ground
in the early nineteenth
century.

labourer named John Harris stole a sheep worth ten pence. He was ordered to be flogged – but was allowed to join the army instead (Childs, pp.113–14). In 1695 the passage of minor criminals into the services was to some extent formalised by the passing of an Act for the Relief of Poor Prisoners for Debt or Damage, which allowed men under forty years old who were imprisoned for debt to be released on condition that they joined either the army or the navy for the duration of the war with France.

There were some in England who held the view that the army was becoming a dumping ground for social misfits of all kinds (on occasion even deserters from foreign armies were welcomed); but the need for recruits continued, whatever the means employed, and the situation changed little in the opening years of the eighteenth century. From 1702 to 1713 England was engaged in the War of the Spanish Succession, and the call for men to fill the ranks was endless. Commanding Officers of regiments bickered over allegations of stealing each other's recruits, and the 'ill-practices of some officers Employed in Recruiting' was mentioned in a document when the Board of General Officers met in February 1705; but the reality which underlay these indications of concern was quite simply that not enough men were coming forward to serve. In 1708 out of a requirement of 18,657 men only 868 had been recruited, and of these thirty-seven were volunteers and the remainder were pressed. (See R.E. Scouller, *The Armies of Queen Anne*, 1966.) The profession of arms was not a popular one and common soldiers, once they had fought their battles, were given scant regard by society at large. Ned Ward, a popular journalist in Queen Anne's reign, was almost certainly expressing a widely held view when he described an infantryman, in *The London Spy* (viii, 1700), in the following terms:

A Foot Soldier is commonly a Man, who for the sake of wearing a Sword, and the Honour of being term'd a Gentleman, is Coax'd from a Handicraft Trade, whereby he might Live Comfortably, to bear Arms, for his King and Country, whereby he has hopes of nothing but to live Starvingly. His Lodging is as near Heaven as his Quarters can raise him; and his Soul generally as near Hell as a Profligate Life can sink him; for to speak without Swearing, he thinks is a Scandal to his Post . . . He often leads a Sober Life against his Will; and when ever he gets Drunk, it is in a Bawdy-House . . . He is generally belov'd by two sorts of Companions, viz. Whores and Lice; for both these Vermin are great Admirers of a Scarlet Coat . . . If he spends twenty Years in Wars and lives to be Forty, perhaps he may get a Halbert [i.e. be promoted Sergeant]; and if he survives Three-score an Hospital . . .

> To a Coblers Aul, or Butchers Knife,
> Or Porter's Knot, commend me;
> But from a Soldier's Lazy Life,
> Good Heaven, I pray, defend me.

Ward again wrote about the army in a pamphlet entitled *Mars Stript of his Armour* which was published in 1708. He repeats the view that the common soldier was seriously underpaid, but it is his description of a captain on recruiting duty that seems to have a ring of truth:

> In charge of recruiting men, he will collect a parcel of poor tradesmen, entertain them at a tavern till they are drunk, cram a shilling in their pockets, and the next morning both he and the sergeant will swear that they were fairly enlisted. – quoted in H.W. Troyer, *Ned Ward of Grub Street*, 1946; 1968.

Varying enlistment procedures – and even those where some form of trickery was involved – did not necessarily have a predictable outcome. Sampson Staniforth, who was born in 1720, went carousing with a friend who was a soldier on leave. He was tricked into enlisting, and his mother intervened to buy him off the following morning; but her efforts were unavailing, for he went off to re-enlist about a week later. Staniforth provides us with one of the few accounts we have of other rank life at a home station in the eighteenth century. He was sent to Edinburgh where 'there were no barracks then, but we lay on straw in a vault, and throughout the winter had but one fire for seventy men.' John Nelson, at this period, had little choice – he was pressed into the army for preaching Methodism, but in fact went on to become a successful soldier and later an even more successful preacher. Thomas Rankin of Dunbar, on the other hand, was impressed as an adolescent by the serious demeanour and good behaviour of a group of dragoons stationed in the town. They had hired a room for prayer and preaching, and were apparently Methodists. The story of Samuel Hutton (born 1733) is that of a willing volunteer. After a period as a vagrant he attempted to join up, but was turned down by the Navy and by several recruiting sergeants on the grounds that he was too short. Eventually, however, a sergeant of the 12th Foot (the Suffolk Regiment) took him because he seemed to be 'a growing lad and would grow taller'. Hutton enlisted at Portsmouth into a regiment which was stationed in Scotland, and since recruits were not due to be sent for some time the sergeant gave him into the care of a landlady with instructions to feed him well. Over a period of sixteen weeks he was given beef and cabbage three times a day! He put on an inch in height and was able to serve successfully with the 12th.

Once a man had joined the army it was perhaps of little concern to him that he might be referred to as 'the refuse and dregs of society', but the treatment often accorded him before he joined his regiment could be (unlike the experience of Samuel Hutton) quite horrifying, and this he would have resented. In London, for example, new recruits were lodged in the Savoy or in the Tower. Ned Ward, in the pamphlet mentioned earlier, was emphatic: 'I dare aver', he wrote, 'that the hardships sustain'd by poor wretches in the Savoy and the Tower, have deterr'd greater numbers from entering into the Service than all the conquests have persuaded to take up arms.' The new soldier invariably 'far'd hard and lodg'd ill', and in 1703 the bad treatment of recruits in the Savoy was the subject of enquiries by a government minister.

Some of the contemporary comment recalled here relates to a period when war was in progress. At this point it should be stressed that recruiting went on in times of peace and of war, even though the procedures were given an especial intensity during periods of armed conflict when the need for more and more men became increasingly urgent. It should also be remembered that during the entire period covered by this book, war and active service have offered to some soldiers opportunities for promotion and advancement that were impossible within the smaller establishments of peacetime armies. By the same token, when contraction of the army took place after a period of war, disbandment of regiments, surpluses of trained officers, non-commissioned officers and men created problems – but they did not, I believe, radically alter the kind of military life and experience discussed in these pages.

An anonymous writer who described himself as 'a Lover of his Country and the Army' tackled the subject of recruiting in a pamphlet entitled *An Essay on the most effective way to Recruit the Army*. It was published in 1707 – a time of war – and made two important points. A major reason for lack of men coming forward to join the army was, the pamphlet said, the simple one of low pay. (Why, asked Daniel Defoe, should anyone volunteer to go overseas and 'be knock'd on the head at the tune of three shillings and six pence a week'?) A second problem, which might at first seem surprising, was the payment of levy money or bounty, which was set at this period at £2 sterling – a not inconsiderable sum, even with deductions. This, said the author, did more harm than good, since men enlisted for the money, got drunk and then deserted. One man called Taylor, condemned for desertion, claimed that he had made over £60 in one year from fraudulent enlistments. Whatever value we attach to the arguments put forward in this pamphlet, they do present the views of one contemporary who clearly sought to solve some of the recruiting problems of the army. From this period, however, such voices are comparatively rare. Too many Englishmen were prepared to agree with Joseph Addison, who stated in his pamphlet *The Present State of the War* (Preface dated

1707), that 'There is not a more disagreeable thought to the people of Great Britain than that of a standing army.' If articulate voices were few, those of the inarticulate common soldiers are virtually non-existent, and we have little idea of how the men in the ranks of Queen Anne's army perceived themselves. The best and most sympathetic assessment of them was made by Major R.E. Scouller, who wrote in these terms:

> . . . when danger had passed, they were looked on as criminals with the additional disadvantage that they were not safely behind bars. Yet, when their loyalty was tried, they performed feats of skill-at-arms, of marching, and of sheer straightforward courage not to be equalled. – *The Armies of Queen Anne*, p.xiv.

The instructions for recruiting which were sent by his Commanding Officer to Captain Sir Henry Seton of the 17th Foot (later the Leicestershire, now the Royal Leicestershire Regiment) throw some light upon procedures at a later period of the eighteenth century, when there are signs that standardisation was beginning to make a tentative appearance in army organisation. Certain categories of men were barred: Frenchmen, deserters, Welshmen, miners and the inhabitants of seaports (who were, presumably, reserved for the attention of naval press gangs). Enlistment was for life, and the age range was from fifteen to twenty-five years, the minimum height being five feet five inches. All recruits were to be examined by a civilian doctor, and the specific disabilities mentioned are ruptures, convulsions and the deformity of being 'baker kneed' (a weakness of the knees connected with bakers' having to stoop to pick up loaded trays). Mention was made earlier of 'necesssaries' which had to be purchased out of the bounty, and they comprised the following items:

	£ s. d.
2 new Shirts about 5/8 each	11 4
1 Black Hair Stock (this to be given him when he joins the Regiment)	8
1 pair of new Shoes	5 0
1 pair of strong white thread stockings, knit, about	3 0
	£1 0 0

Sometimes recruiting officers were just unlucky. Captain Delacherois of the 9th Regiment (later the Royal Norfolks) was sent from Ireland where he was stationed to England on recruiting duties. He travelled from Swansea to Pylle and Bristol in the summer of 1770, and then on to Wells, 'a handsome, pleasing but retired town', he wrote, 'inhabited by parsons, superannuated coachmen and postboys.' He had hopes of picking up volunteers at Shepton Mallet, where he stayed for a week, but men were scarce because of the harvest. By August he had gathered only nine recruits, four of whom deserted; and of the remainder all save one were turned down on their arrival at regimental headquarters in Ireland. He sent another man who deserted as soon as he landed in Cork, so Delacherois lost altogether something over £15. He was equally unsuc-

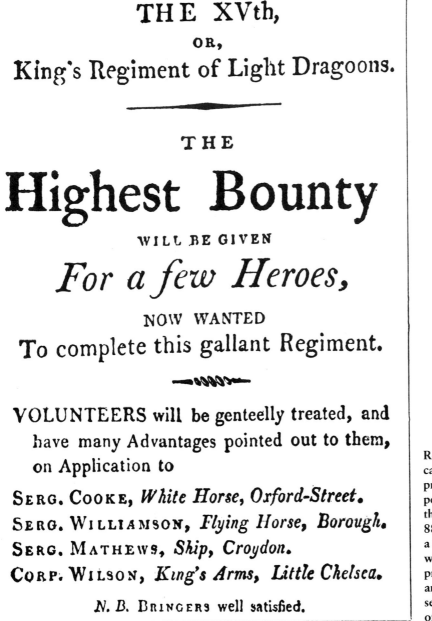

THE XVth,

OR,

King's Regiment of Light Dragoons.

THE

Highest Bounty

WILL BE GIVEN

For a few Heroes,

NOW WANTED

To complete this gallant Regiment.

VOLUNTEERS will be genteelly treated, and have many Advantages pointed out to them, on Application to

SERG. COOKE, *White Horse, Oxford-Street.*

SERG. WILLIAMSON, *Flying Horse, Borough.*

SERG. MATHEWS, *Ship, Croydon.*

CORP. WILSON, *King's Arms, Little Chelsea.*

N. B. BRINGERS well satisfied.

Recruiting poster for a cavalry regiment. It probably dates from the period 1769–1807. Like the earlier poster for the 88th, it mentions 'bringers', a reference to the crimps who made a living by procuring potential recruits and delivering them to sergeants for the formalities of enlistment.

cessful as he went north to Worcester and Kidderminster, then on to Stourbridge and Bridgnorth. By April 1771 he was back with his regiment in Ireland.

If the experience of this unfortunate recruiter was in any way typical, it is hardly surprising that recourse was had to less legal though traditional methods of raising men. The army was chronically short of soldiers – some 10,000 below strength in 1758, for instance – and the activities of men like Michael Tooley ('crimps', as they came to be called) became more widespread. Crimps were the middlemen in recruiting. They trafficked in eligible men and found soldiers for hard-pressed recruiting officers and sergeants. The anonymous author of a pamphlet, *Reflections on the Pernicious Custom of Recruiting by Crimps* published towards the end of the eighteenth century, described their activities:

> I know the truth of the existence of Crimps by experience, that I can point out the houses and the names of persons by whom men have been bought and sold; where you might have gone and chosen men as you would hogs or horses, according to their size, their make, their ages, and their appearing; some for eight, ten, twelve guineas; and now I am told that the price is raised to more than twenty guineas for fine young men.

If authority turned a blind eye to these practices, ordinary citizens did not always do so. We have seen this in the case of Tooley, and the *Register of the Times*, April 1795, reported the following incident:

> A very serious riot had like to have happened late on the evening of the 14th inst. in Charles Street Westminster: the circumstances are as follows: a kidnapping sergeant, about seven, was passing along Newman-street, Oxford-road, and perceiving a youth, about fifteen come out of a tradesman's house (which it has since appeared was his master's) the crimp followed him, and desired he would take a shilling and purchase some tobacco at a shop close by; the unsuspecting youth did it, and when he returned, the fellow immediately seized him, and told him he had taken the King's money, and must go for a gentleman soldier. He was in the act of dragging him away, when the boy, by his cries alarmed the whole neighbourhood, who flew to his assistance and rescued him. They seized the kidnapper, and gave him over to the mob, who calmly heard the story, and then took him to the next pump, and attempted to purify him with water . . .

Despite the use of the description 'crimp', this story appears to be another account of trickery into 'taking the shilling'. Nevertheless crimps, as middlemen, managed to maintain a steady supply of men by offering potential recruits cash in hand. Another of their activities was instruction in the art of enlisting and deserting over and over again so that quite considerable sums of money could be made. Occasionally one comes across striking examples of fraudulent enlistment. On 21 April 1787 (according to G.R. Clarke in *The History and Topography of Ipswich*, 1830), a Richard Kedgson was hanged at Rushmore, near Ipswich, after confessing at his trial that he had enlisted forty-nine times into different regiments in England, Scotland and Ireland. Reference was made earlier to a claim early in the eighteenth century that £60 had been obtained in this way. When we come to Kedgson later in the century, his claim was that he had received no less than 397 guineas in bounty payments. *The Chelmsford Chronicle* dated 7 December 1787 reported the death of a London man known as 'Tom the Devil', who had enlisted into upwards of thirty regiments and nearly as many militia units, and had deserted from them all. On one occasion, it was said, he had been drummed out of the Guards.

It is a matter of regret that, so far as I am aware, no one who was involved in crimping wrote about his experiences. A much odder case than those connected with crimping was that of Sergeant Graves of the 87th Foot (later Royal Irish Fusiliers) who, according to *Aris's Birmingham Gazette* of 17 February 1794, deserted from the army taking with him two men called Jesson and Rew whom he had enlisted in Birmingham. What on earth can have possessed Graves to desert? As a recruiter he was in a position of trust, and he was an experienced soldier, having earlier served in the 10th Foot (Royal Lincolnshire Regiment). All we can say is that at this period the system of recruiting was chaotic; and eventually, in 1796, Parliament passed a Bill which began to regularise recruiting procedures.

The earliest account of a volunteer recruit's early days in the army is that of Sergeant Roger Lamb, who joined the 9th Foot in Dublin in 1773. 'During twenty-one days', he wrote in the *Memoir of His Own Life* 'I was drilled for four hours each day.' Only when he had achieved some proficiency was he issued with a set of accoutrements, a firelock musket so that he could proceed to arms drill. Some of the old drill sergeants, said Lamb, were unnecessarily severe. William Cobbett, who enlisted a little later in 1784, looked back at the inadequacy of army pay. Out of six pence per day he had to buy both food and cleaning materials. 'Judge then', he wrote, 'of the quantity of food to sustain life in a lad of sixteen to enable him to exercise with a musket six to eight hours every day.' A number of men deserted out of sheer hunger. Cobbett endured the hardships and was fairly soon promoted Corporal, for which he was paid two pence extra a day and wore 'a very clever worsted knot' at the shoulder to show his new rank.

One other example of an enlistment at this point is interesting because although Joseph Mayett, a Buckinghamshire labourer, joined the militia (not the regular army) at the beginning of the nineteenth century during the Napoleonic invasion scare, his reasons for doing so may well have been fairly typical. At church in Buckingham he saw a number of redcoats: they were 'Sergeants and Corporals and musick men and all very Clean I was much delighted to see them and hear the musick.' Within a day or two he joined up and spent eight hours a day, for an unspecified period, in Aylesbury doing his recruit's training. He served until 1815, when he was discharged. (See *The Autobiography of Joseph Mayett of Quainton*, edited by Ann Kussmaul, Buckinghamshire Record Society No. 23, 1986.)

This was the year which marked the beginning of a long pause in Britain's military involvement on the European mainland which lasted, with the exception of the Crimean War, for something like a century. Not until 1914 were British armies actively deployed in Europe. The long period of peace – always excepting colonial wars and imperial adventures – which followed 1815 meant that recruiting, although a constant process, was no longer so pressing as it had been throughout the eighteenth century. Attempts had been made as early as 1796, as we have seen, to regularise procedures, and by the end of the Napoleonic Wars the army was for the time being more inclined to shed men than to recruit on a large scale. There were other factors which worked, indirectly but effectively,

A group of recruiting sergeants outside the National Gallery, London, in the 1890s. Each is from a different regiment; one, distinguished by his sabre and spurs, is from the cavalry. Considerable rivalry would exist between them, and they would outbid each other for the allegiance of the man who is making up his mind.

against illegal methods of recruiting, and some which provided an incentive for men to become soldiers.

The industrial revolution saw the rise of a working class, many of whom were less likely to regard themselves as hapless victims of fate, of employers or of crimping agents than their eighteenth-century forbears had been. Many working men, through what was often self-education, had developed new sensibilities and a new awareness of the world in which they found themselves. This does not mean, of course, that poverty and unemployment were not potent recruiting agents; nor does it deny that some – many, indeed – soldiers were like Noah Claypole's father in Charles Dickens' *Oliver Twist*, described as 'drunken', who ended up with a wooden leg and a pension of two and a half pence per day; but it does mean that more men who were both articulate and literate joined the army in the nineteenth century. They were not Kipling's 'Gentlemen Rankers', the 'lost ones' as he described them. Most soldiers were drawn from the working class, driven by various compulsions to enlist; a few, probably drawn from what Geoffrey Best called the 'flag-waving, foreigner-hating, peer-loving side of the plebeian mind', were determined to make something of an army career. There were sound reasons why they should do so.

In its imperial role, policing the empire, the army was not altogether unattractive to recruits. Even the private soldier in India or elsewhere in the colonies enjoyed, when he was not on active service, a more comfortable life than the one he would have had as a civilian at home where tedium and boredom in repetitive, unskilled jobs were rewarded with low wages, slum living conditions and the ever present threat of unemployment. For many men the undoubted tedium of garrison life was easier to bear, and there was always the perceived attraction of wearing a uniform.

Another factor – and one about which we have much to learn – was the need of the army for increasingly large numbers of skilled non-commissioned and warrant officers. Serving soldiers who achieved rank because they were skilled military tradesmen created a great leaven in the ranks, besides offering the beginnings of a varied career structure to able men who enlisted. A standard guide to the army (O.L. Perry, *Rank and Badges* . . ., 2nd Edition, 1888) gives a reliable idea of the ranks and duties which were open: they included Conductors of Supplies and of Stores; Sergeant-Major Foreman of Works; Sergeant-Major Mechanist; several grades of Instructor and Master-Gunner; Sergeant Farrier. Trumpeters, Buglers and Drummers might reach Sergeant's rank, and below that there was a variety of specialist jobs for corporals. There was even a rank of Sergeant Photographer . . . and of course a range of ranks and appointments connected with pay offices and orderly rooms. In addition to such 'departmental' posts there was a larger establishment of Sergeants-Major and Quartermasters in infantry, cavalry and artillery units.

Nevertheless, the prejudice against the army showed little sign of disappearing, and the reasons why men joined up remain uncertain. In an account of his service, *Camp and Barrack Room: or, the British Army as it is*, published in 1846, Staff Sergeant J. MacMullen of the 13th Light

Recruits for the 55th Regiment, Ireland, 1854.

25

Infantry (later the Somerset Light Infantry) provided details of why one hundred and twenty of his fellow soldiers had enlisted. The majority, two-thirds in fact, had been unemployed; two were respectable men who had fallen on hard times; sixteen thought the army was an easy life; eight were shady characters who regarded soldiering as the last resort; there was one criminal; two men had fallen out with their families; eight were discontented with civilian life; one was ambitious; and the remaining two gave no reason. For the year 1839, roughly the same period as that covered by MacMullen, Colonel H.C.B. Cook published in the *Journal of the Society for Army Historical Research* in Autumn 1971 details of enlistments into the 80th Foot (later the South Staffordshire Regiment) showing the districts from which recruits came, their civilian trades and what happened to the men. At the time the regiment was stationed in New South Wales and its depot where recruits were gathered was at Chatham.

PLACE OF ORIGIN

Middlesex (including London)	27	Other English Counties	18
Staffordshire	13	Southern Irish	6
Surrey	9	Northern Irish	5
Kent	7	Scots	3
Cambridgeshire	7	Welsh	1
Rutland	7		
Lincolnshire	4		
Northamptonshire	3		
Sussex	3		

TRADES		WHAT BECAME OF THEM	
Labourers	64	Died	48
Servants	9	Discharged	30
Tailors	6	Killed in action	9
Potters	6	"Volunteered"	8
Colliers	4	Deserted	7
Others	24	Transferred	7
		Invalided	3
		Promoted Quartermaster	1

While the regiment clearly maintained a link with Staffordshire, it is clear that most of the recruits came from areas not too far from the depot. The numbers of men from Cambridgeshire and Rutland suggest that a recruiting party had been active in that area. The majority of the enlistments were from the lower strata of society. The high death rate would be because the regiment went to Burma, and those killed in action nearly all fell in the first Sikh War. The transfers were mainly to the New South Wales Mounted Police, and the 'volunteers' were men who opted to transfer to other regiments in order to stay in India. The man promoted Quartermaster was a labourer from Tipperary. What is striking is the low desertion rate – the temptation for young soldiers on detachment in Australia to desert and 'take to the bush' must have been considerable.

At about this time, Staff Sergeant MacMullen was doing his recruit training at Rochester, and his experiences are typical in many respects of what other young men who joined the army at this period went through:

> Probably some readers may wish to know the daily routine of my duties and amusements at this period. I rose at five o'clock in the morning, and made up my bed; which occupied at least a quarter of an hour, and was rather a troublesome job. I then made my toilet, and at six turned out for drill, from which we were dismissed at a quarter to eight, when we breakfasted. From ten till twelve we were again at drill; had dinner at one, in the shape of potatoes and meat, both usually of the most wretched quality; and at two fell in for another drill, which terminated at four; after which hour my time was at my own disposal until tattoo, provided I was not ordered on piquet. During this period of leisure I generally amused myself by strolling in the vicinity of the garrison (no soldier being permitted to go a greater distance than one mile) or by reading . . .

Many of his contemporaries, one suspects, would have spent their leisure time drinking, but MacMullen was very highly motivated and wrote about the value of garrison libraries as a means of keeping men out of what he called the 'beer-shop'. When he was a recruit, however, there was no such institution, and he had to borrow the books he read from a circulating library in town. He did see the establishment of garrison libraries during his service.

The experience of men going into the army later in the nineteenth century is much better documented than it is for the earlier years. In an important respect terms of service had changed: enlistment was no longer for life, and soldiers with a satisfactory record of eighteen years' service became eligible for the award of a long service and good conduct medal – the 'rooty-gong' in army slang. Some might go on to complete what they called their 'pontoon', twenty-one years' service. One of the shrewdest observers of such changes was Trooper William Robertson of the 16th (Queen's) Lancers. He went on to become a Field Marshal – the only man in the army of whom it was said that he had served in every rank. He joined his regiment in Aldershot in November 1877 and his autobiography, *From Private to Field Marshal*, was published in 1921:

> The life of a recruit in 1877 was a very different matter from what it is now (1921). The system introduced in 1871–72 by Mr Cardwell – one of the greatest War Ministers the country has ever had – under which men enlisted for twelve years' service (six years full time and six on the Regular Reserve) had not yet had time to get into full swing. Regiments were, therefore, still composed mainly of old soldiers who, although very admirable comrades in some respects and with a commendable code of honour of their own, were in many cases – not in all – addicted to rough behaviour, heavy drinking, and hard swearing. They could not well be blamed for this. Year in and year out they went through the same routine, were treated like machines of an inferior kind – and having little prospect of finding employment on the expiration of their twenty-one years engagement, they lived only for the present, the single bright spot in their existence being the receipt of a few shillings – perhaps not more than one – on the weekly pay-day. These rugged veterans exacted full deference from the

recruit, who was assigned the worst bed in the room, given the smallest amount of food and the least palatable, had to 'lend' them articles of kit which they had lost or sold, 'fag' for them in a variety of ways, and, finally, was expected to share with them at the regimental canteen such cash as he might have in the purchase of beer sold at 3d. a quart.

Another view of a recruit's experience in late Victorian England is provided by Robert Blatchford, who achieved fame as author of the bestseller *Merry England* (1893) and was for many years editor of the socialist weekly magazine *Clarion*. He became a soldier in the 103rd Regiment (Royal Dublin Fusiliers) in 1881 – the year in which numbered regiments were given specific names. 'I *had* to go for a soldier . . . ', he wrote in the first chapter of his *My Life in the Army* (1910); and his enthusiasm for the army pervades the book and was, in the end, to play a major part in his break with the socialist movement which, as a journalist, he had done so much to promote. He enlisted in London and spent his first night in the receiving room at St George's Barracks. 'Here', he wrote, 'was a great bare room, with bed-cots down each side, as in a hospital ward, and gas-lights flaring overhead.' He and the other recruits were roused at six the following morning and, after a cold-water wash, taken before a doctor. Of the forty men in his party destined for various units, six failed to pass the medical examination and the remainder were taken to a police court, where they were formally sworn in as soldiers, at sixteen pence per day with deductions for groceries. Next day the fourteen recruits destined for the 103rd were marched to Waterloo Station for a train to Southampton, then a boat to the Isle of Wight where the regiment was stationed. On the pier at Cowes – Blatchford, oddly, does not mention an escorting corporal – the party was met by a Staff Sergeant who led them to the barracks at Parkhurst. On the following day the party was examined by the regimental doctor, who rejected two men as unfit. The remaining twelve were issued with kit, posted to companies, and their training began.

Not all the training was of a formal nature. Early on, Blatchford struck up an acquaintance with Pompey Pride, a private soldier of some years' standing, because they had adjoining beds in the barrack room and became, as the saying was, 'cot-mates'. Pompey instructed Blatchford in the best way to clean his kit – 'Don't put the pipeclay in thick', he adjured – and gave him practical tips on behaviour in barracks. The formal training was more demanding:

> It was very cold when we turned out for our first recruits' drill at six o'clock one morning. We . . . were new men in our scarlet serge jackets, glengarry caps, and regulation boots. We were handed over first of all to a corporal, who took us to the gymnasium. Here we put on canvas shoes and belts, and hung up our caps and tunics. Then a short, red-headed, crabby gymnastic sergeant came and looked us over; after which a corporal formed us into fours and led us in a run of one thousand yards round a field. This over, we went to dumb-bells and parallel bars . . . This over, we re-dressed and with aching limbs and rather dizzy heads ran back to breakfast.

An early nineteenth-century drill sergeant and (OPPOSITE) the recruits he is instructing.

After breakfast the recruits were handed over to drill instructors. The new soldiers, Blatchford recalled, were kept 'pretty busy . . . at drill, or school, or gymnasium from six in the morning to six in the evening.' After parade there were arms and equipment to clean and tables to be scrubbed. Blatchford's summing up of his few weeks of basic training spoke, I believe, for many other recruits, at different periods, who were less articulate than he was:

> But we were young and the air was good. And the gymnastics, the drilling, and the regular hours and plain food began to tell. In a few weeks we were straight and smart, and stood and moved lightly. In the bronzed, alert, upright young soldiers no one could have recognised the mob of assorted ragamuffins who had tramped in the dust from Cowes . . . Indeed, we began to be rather proud of ourselves, and imagine we were soldiers.

Another writer who became in his day a household word – 'It is impossible not to be thrilled by Edgar Wallace', it was said – joined the army in 1893 at the age of eighteen. Down on his luck, he borrowed six pence to pay his fare to Woolwich and enlisted for seven years' service with the Royal West Kent Regiment. On arrival at Maidstone Barracks he was taken to his quarters, 'a long bare room' whose only occupant was a soldier engaged in polishing buttons and cleaning equipment which lay all over his bed, in preparation for guard duty. An 'old sweat', he had served for seven years and re-enlisted for a further five. He liked India, there was no place like it; but the army, he confided, was not what it was! Wallace soon became involved in the daily routine. 'For days', he wrote in his autobiography *People*, published in 1926, 'I moved like a man in a dream. I drew my kit, was measured for my scarlet coat, possessed myself of a rifle and bayonet and . . . equipment.' He also learned to distinguish the bugle calls by which a soldier's life in barracks was regulated. He found his training interesting, but eventually, as we shall see, he transferred to the Medical Staff Corps.

Army reforms at this period were moving slowly. Enlightened statesmen like Cardwell and Haldane did much to improve conditions of service, and even to increase pay – though not by very much. The six regular divisions making up the British Expeditionary Force which landed in France in August 1914 was said to be the best organised and best equipped force ever to leave the shores of Britain for active service.

The war gave a tremendous stimulus to voluntary recruiting. Even so, the inexorable demands of trench warfare was to render this system inadequate, and so for the first time in its history Britain had recourse to conscription. The first Military Service Act which became law in January 1916 made liable for service all single men and childless widowers between the ages of eighteen and forty-one. It was amended by six further Acts. The act of 1918 permitted the extension of compulsory service for men up to the age of fifty-six, and the final one, passed in April 1919, retained conscription for a further twelve months. Altogether more than five and a half million men served in the British Army during the war. At the outbreak it consisted, with reserves and part-time Territorials, of 733,

514 men. Between August 1914 and December 1915 enlistments numbered 2,466,719, and conscription between January 1916 and November 1918 brought in 2,504,183 men. Never before had the army had to cope with such numbers, and they placed an obvious strain on the military machine.

So far as recruiting was concerned, the years 1914 and 1915 were full of interest when we look at the methods used to induce men to join up and the moral climate in which such pressures and persuasions were employed. There were specialised appeals to such groups as sportsmen, stockbrokers, tramway workers, railway men and others to join up together and form their own units. There were 'pals' battalions, particularly favoured in the industrial areas, where enlistment was based upon men from streets and localities who were assured that they would be able to serve together. Altogether 115 infantry battalions were raised in this way. The advantage of the system was that the men knew each other. The converse was that when a regiment incurred very heavy casualties, whole streets in a town could be devastated by the loss of their men in one engagement. For men who would otherwise have been ineligible for service because they could not satisfy the requirements of minimum height, there were specially formed 'bantam' battalions. A good deal of emphasis was placed upon local effort, and committees set up and run by members of local establishments throughout the land were active. Typical of regional recruiting campaigns was one at Preston, Lancashire, in August 1915. It featured marching bands, pipers, a 'moving picture' van, fêtes, garden parties, and much was made of a local man who had won the Victoria Cross. Exhortation was the order of the day: 'We don't want to lose you, but we think you *ought* to go', ran the words of a popular song at this period. The watchword in these early months of the war was patriotism, and the phrase 'For King and Country' was freely bandied about. Organised religion played its part. The influence of the clergy was almost unequivocal: they supported the war, and in many ways actively promoted recruiting. Although the Archbishop of Canterbury refused to sanction the use of pulpit for such a purpose, other diocesan bishops were energetic in their efforts to raise men. The Bishop of London, in particular, did much to popularise the notion that Britain was engaged in a 'holy war' against the forces of evil. The Dean of Ripon was outspoken: 'The Lord', he declared, 'is on our side'; while another clergyman, looking at the armed conflict with its myriad dead and wounded, remarked: 'We watch the Divine Artificer at work.' Such views were, in all probability, more widely held than we might think – but the clergymen who gave voice to them are unlikely to have had much in common with those regimental chaplains of all denominations who showed remarkable courage in ministering to soldiers in the front line.

The realities of trench warfare were not at first realised by the public at large, and popular newspapers did little to make them known. Besides the chauvinism which pervaded their columns there was a tight censorship, and the activities and reports of journalists in France and Belgium were rigidly controlled. Popular artists like R. Caton Woodville presented a

F·H·Townsend 1915

hcroic and patriotic image of the fighting in the pages of topical maga-
zines. Death was made acceptable in a world of patriotic gallantry,
determination and self-sacrifice, and pictures depicting such values in
terms of battle reached a wide public. It is also true to say that the men
who experienced the fighting on the Western Front lacked, for the most
part, the ability to describe what they had seen – and in any case, their
letters home were censored. It is little wonder, then, that voluntary
recruiting for the army proceeded until the end of 1915 in an atmosphere
which fed upon half-truth and dubious exhortation not unmixed with
idealism. They were, initially at least, heady days of a popular rush to the
colours.

One of the men who had volunteered at this time was Private Cook – a
hospital clerk in civilian life – who joined the 3rd Battalion, East Surrey
Regiment, when it was stationed at Dover in a tented camp on the Western
Heights above the town. It is thanks to him that we are able to glimpse
something of what happened to those who enlisted in the early days of the
war. He wrote to his family throughout his service, and his son used some
of the earlier letters (there were two hundred and ninety in all) in an article
published in the *Journal of the Society for Army Historical Research*, Vol.
LXV No. 264 (Winter 1987). Among his fellow recruits were a schoolmaster, a traveller, an interpreter, a postman and a 'gentleman's son' from
Richmond – 'rather too much of a toff for some of the others, but I get on
all right with him', wrote Cook. Food was described as satisfactory, and it
was possible to purchase 'extras' from the Royal Victoria Home for

In this unusually barbed
Punch cartoon, the
recruiting officer who has
asked a thirteen-year-old
boy pretending to be
sixteen, 'Do you know
where boys go who tell
lies?' is given the straight
answer, 'To the Front, Sir.'
Under-age enlistment was
common in the first
eighteen months or so of
the Great War.

Exhibition of recruiting posters held at the Central London Recruiting Office, New Scotland Yard, in 1938.

Soldiers near the camp. Because there was a shortage of khaki uniforms with the influx of so many men into the army, the uniforms issued were blue – and Cook mentions others who wore red. It was not until 17 January 1915 that he received a khaki uniform, which was loose round the neck and slack round the waist but, as he said, it looked more like the real thing. Throughout Cook's early weeks in the army the weather wreaked havoc with the basic training schedule and with the tents in which they lived. On 12 November 1914 the unit moved into Old Mill Barracks in Nargate Street, and it was here that he was selected for training as a machine gunner.

In the end, however, the voluntary system proved to be inadequate. War-weariness, cynicism of the kind hinted at by C.E. Montague in his book *Disenchantment* (1922), and an increasing sense of reality occasioned by lengthening casualty lists all led to a fall in the number of men volunteering. Thus conscription became necessary. It was dropped after the war, and the unemployment which was widespread in the 1920s and 1930s provided a constant pool of men from whom volunteers came forward. Conscription was reintroduced in 1939, some months before the outbreak of the Second World War, and did not end until 1963. During the war, volunteering for the army before official 'call-up' was for most applicants a matter offering little choice. One could join the infantry in one of a number of 70th (Young Soldiers) Battalions recruited by some county regiments. For older men there were 30th (Home Service) Battalions. Such units were, however, disbanded in the later months of 1942. Conscripts who underwent selection tests were very much better off in regard to the branch of the army in which they might serve.

Ironically perhaps, it was the conscripts of the period from 1945 to 1963 who were most articulate about their period of service. In his book,

The Best Years of their Lives (1986), Trevor Royle presents a convincing portrait of conscript life by allowing many of the men concerned to speak for themselves. Since for every naval conscript there were twelve for the Royal Air Force while the army took thirty-three, this book is mostly about soldiers. One of them, Denis Gane, who later became a corporal in the Royal Corps of Signals, noted that 'the transition from civilian to soldier was dramatic both in its speed and effect.'

Recruits joined a training unit on a Thursday and the following three days were spent in medical inspection, innoculation, kitting out. On the following Monday their training began. They had a long day which began with Reveille, usually at 6.15 or 6.30 a.m.; breakfast was at about 7.00, and the day's work began after a muster parade at 8.00 or 8.15. Drill, physical training, fieldcraft, lectures, weapon training . . . and there were also periods spent on education, as well as firing of weapons on the range. Tea, the last meal of the day, was at about 5.00, and evenings were spent in cleaning kit for the following day and perhaps visiting the NAAFI canteen where hot meals and beverages could be purchased. It goes without saying that barrack rooms had to be kept clean at all times – recruits and their quarters were always subject to inspection. After tea, beds could be 'made down' (as the army phrase had it) ready for sleeping – they were required to be made daily with blankets in a neat pile, surrounded by items of kit and spare boots. Lights Out was sounded at 10.30. It was, in the early weeks, a tough life for new soldiers, but it almost always became somewhat easier when, with their basic training successfully completed, they were posted to their units.

It is difficult to arrive at any balanced assessment of peacetime conscription. More than twenty-five years later tales are still told about bullying non-commissioned officers, whitewashing coal, weeding lawns with a knife and fork (knife, fork and spoon – 'eating irons' – were a personal issue to every soldier when he joined up). Boredom and waste of time are still recalled. On the other hand there are happy memories of comradeship, laughable incidents . . . there were some who enjoyed being soldiers, and even those who did not will sometimes admit that they gained something from their two years of service.

Since the return to a voluntary army in 1963 recruiting has become a very much more sophisticated process than it has ever been before. Gone are the days when any vagabond or petty criminal could take the King's (or Queen's) shilling with no questions asked. Unlike Sergeant Kite, the present day recruiter works from one of the forty-one main Army Careers Information Offices scattered throughout the country. It will be in such an office that a young man or young woman who thinks of joining up will make first enquiries. The recruiting sergeant on secondment from his regiment will talk to the candidate and assess his or her suitability for army life, stressing the 'three Ds: danger, discipline and discomfort' which characterise a soldier's life. Applicants are then interviewed by an officer who has usually retired from the active list, to check that he agrees with the sergeant's initial assessment. If he does, there follows an invitation to attend a twenty-four-hour selection probe at the Army Personnel Selection

Centre at Sutton Coldfield, Warwickshire, or women applicants go to the Women's Royal Army Corps Depot at Guildford, Surrey, or to the Queen Alexandra's Royal Army Nursing Corps at Aldershot. A sub-unit of the Sutton Coldfield centre operates in Edinburgh for Scottish candidates.

At this stage some fifteen per cent of applicants drop out. The applicants will be told precisely what the initial enlistment of probably three years entails, and also what vacancies there are in various branches of the army. An attempt is always made to accommodate individual preferences where possible, and there are aptitude and physical tests, interviews, opportunities to talk with serving soldiers. The potential recruits return home, and those whose applications are successful attend later at the Information Office to take an oath of allegiance to Queen and country, a ceremony to which parents may be invited.

One echo of the pressures of earlier times is worth noting. In the year 1985–86 the North East of England, where unemployment was taking so heavy a toll of youthful hopes, was the most fertile ground for army recruiting. There were 6,303 male applications, of whom 1,642 enlisted; 1,633 women applied to join up, and 153 did so. In times of high employment the army can afford to be very selective. Even so, mistakes are made. In such cases, as one commanding officer put it, 'If a man's really unhappy we don't want to keep him and he doesn't have to stay . . .' (Tony Parker, *Soldier, Soldier*, 1985).

Initial training is as demanding as ever. One private soldier who made a success of his service told Tony Parker: 'They shout at you and run you around to see if they can make you feel like getting out. Specially if you try and give it to them that you're tough, then they'll give you a specially hard time . . . ' It should be added, however, that the army offers a wide range of specialist tasks, and provides the training for them. This is an incentive that many find attractive, and a reason, quite apart from the spur to

Recruits for a searchlight unit being issued with their uniforms, *c.* 1938.

It's a

real man's

life

join the
REGULAR ARMY

Apply to any Army Recruiting Office or Employment Exchange, or write to the War Office (M P 6), London, S.W.I

NASH

Recruiting poster, 1951.

applications provided while unemployment is at a high level, why the army can be much more selective than it has ever been about the men and women who are to fill its ranks. Recruits coming into the army will find a degree of elitism which, although somewhat less obvious than in the past, is still prevalent. There is a hierarchical structure upon which the army necessarily depends, and a tacit acceptance of a class structure – although this can on occasion be surprisingly flexible. Everyone has a place dependent upon rank: Jack, quite clearly, is not seen to be as good as his master. In fact, the army copes remarkably well with many of the human problems which can arise in this kind of society. It is, as it has always been, a society apart; and the appeal to tradition remains potent despite the disbandment, since the end of the war, of so many county regiments which drew upon a deep vein of local sentiment. Relationships between officers, non-commissioned officers and men in the technical arms and amongst parachute troops seem, so far as an outsider can judge, to be more relaxed – though not less formal – than they are in some infantry battalions and in those armoured units which trace their ancestry from the cavalry, which always saw itself as an elite force. The army today derives much of its inner strength from its sense of being a community apart, and this is an attitude which recruits quickly pick up and adopt as their own. Whatever one may think about the political motivations behind the armed conflict in the Falkland Islands in 1982, there is absolutely no doubt at all that the army acquitted itself well.

There is occasional recourse today to KAPE (Keeping the Army in the Public Eye) tours. They feature bands, pipers, buglers and drummers . . . perhaps in some respects the recruiting wheel has come full circle! There has, however, been some unwelcome publicity for the army arising from two recruiting problems which have been given prominence in the late 1980s. First there is the matter of the recruitment of black soldiers. The Prince of Wales has pointed to their absence among troops at ceremonial parades like Trooping the Colour, and to the fact that there are few Blacks serving in the Guards or the Household Cavalry. This is not, says the army emphatically, a matter of policy: the selection computer is colour blind. Altogether there are several thousand black men and women serving, but only a few have reached the rank of sergeant or sergeant-major, and there are fewer still who are officers. Some twenty-five years ago, when there were limitations on the number of Blacks accepted for military training, the quota for the Household Division was nil. Today official recruiting leaflets tell applicants 'The Armed Forces are Equal Opportunity Employers under the terms of the Race Relations Act, 1976.' Clearly something is not as it should be. Computers may be colour blind, but what about the attitudes of those who supply them with data, or of those who select men and women for promotion? Attitudes vary. A sergeant in the Royal Fusiliers summed up what ought to be the accepted one: 'If the guy's watching your back in Northern Ireland and he's good, then you don't give a f — what colour he is.' There is also the story of the black sergeant bugler of the Royal Green Jackets some years ago. He was an outstanding performer and made several records for the army, besides being personally commended by Lord Mountbatten. Yet when his band was invited to appear on the television show Blue Peter, he was relegated to the rear rank which in the event did not go into the studio to be filmed. The short-sightedness – to put it no more critically – of practices like this must, when they become known, do a great deal of damage to the public image of the army and to its ability to recruit the wide range of men and women, regardless of colour, whose skills and enthusiasm are necessary to maintain its efficiency. This is an issue which still causes more than a nagging resentment, and was angrily referred to by a black Member of Parliament in the House of Commons in January 1988.

This intervention by Bernie Grant, the Member concerned, came during a debate which touched on a second problem. It followed a statement by Roger Freeman, Minister for the Armed Forces, that the army was preparing a crack-down on the bullying and intimidation of recruits. Allegations of ill-treatment had been a cause of concern for some time. There had been some very ugly incidents, and a tragic one when an Asian soldier hanged himself. A battalion of the King's Own Scottish Borderers achieved national prominence with stories of 'initiation ceremonies' of a nasty and often degrading kind to which recruits had been subjected by fellow private soldiers of longer service. The scandal was such that the commanding officer was replaced and the regimental sergeant-major posted back to the Scottish depot, and a number of men were court-martialled. Other cases elsewhere in the army came to light, and only a week after the Minister's statement a sergeant was found guilty at a court martial in Shropshire of bullying recruits.

It may be possible to keep a sense of proportion in such matters. There are, said the Minister, 160,000 regulars serving, of whom some 20,000 are under training, and in 1986 and 1987 only 100 cases of alleged bullying, ill-treatment or intimidation had come to light. Of these, nearly half had not been substantiated. Such figures do not, of course, include incidents – or racial abuses – which are never reported . . . All that can be said with certainty is that such episodes reported by the media, to say nothing of rumours and vague allegations, do great damage to public perceptions of the army – and not least, one would have thought, amongst those who might otherwise want to become soldiers.

Soldiers of the Queen's Regiment on patrol in Belfast, August 1988.

Chapter 2

BARRACK DISCIPLINE

Once a recruit had joined the army, he was kitted out and began his initial training. Usually the place of enlistment was some distance from the regiment's station, and in the past this meant that the recruit had to be marched to his unit or, if it was serving abroad, then to a regimental depot. By the mid-nineteenth century he would have gone by train, provided with a travel warrant. Even later, by the turn of the century, recruits would receive their instructions by letter, again with a travel warrant. The common element in all these procedures was the existence of a barracks or a camp where a regiment was stationed or had its depot. Traditionally the initiation of the new recruit into the army was left to corporals, sergeants and sergeants-major. To them fell the task of making soldiers out of an assorted group of civilians – and to a very large extent it still does.

Before the building of barracks in the later eighteenth century – by 1797 forty-nine barracks were in use in the British Isles – soldiers were billeted on civilians, a procedure extremely unpopular with the householders whose homes were used in this way. 'My house', wrote one justifiably irate gentleman in 1647, 'is and hath been full of soldiers this fortnight, such uncivil drinkers and thirsty souls that a barrel of good ale trembles at the sight of them, and the whole house is nothing but a rendezvous of tobacco and spitting.' This system of billeting on local people gradually fell into disuse as more barracks were built, but the old laws relating to the billeting of soldiers in inns remained in force during the Second World War. Even in peacetime, as late as 1935, it was still the custom while the Court was in residence at Windsor for the regiment of Household Cavalry in garrison to supply two Corporals of Horse for duty at the Castle. These non-commissioned officers were invariably billeted at the White Hart and the Castle Hotels.

The building of premises for soldiers to occupy went on right through the nineteenth century. In 1805 about 150,000 troops could be accommodated in 203 separate barracks. The first bath in an English barracks was installed in 1855, but despite this advance in hygiene, conditions in many of them remained extremely poor, and overcrowding presented a serious hazard to health and well-being. George Godwin wrote in 1859: 'The rooms are very confined, the beds are packed in close together, the windows are insufficient and ill-placed; where there are ventilators, they are so actively offensive, that the men risk the unfelt danger and stop them; and thus the soldier sleeps in poison and dies in consequence.' Godwin had in mind barracks in London, but there is no reason to suppose that conditions were better elsewhere.

After the Crimean War, largely in Aldershot, Colchester, Shorncliffe and the Curragh in Ireland, the process of army building accelerated and barracks were much improved. Some of the accommodation built then

Reading Room of St Mary's Barracks, Chatham, 1856. Provision of books and somewhere to read them, or where letters could be written, represented one of the improvements in barrack facilities initiated in the post-Crimean period. Military authorities at all levels were anxious to keep soldiers out of public houses wherever possible.

was still in use during the Second World War. Barrack rooms, in which the men lived with a corporal or a lance-corporal in charge, were quite lofty and had adequate windows. They were heated by a solid-fuel stove and were not, as a rule, overcrowded. Facilities for the men, however, remained rather primitive. In some rooms lockers for kit were provided, but in others there was only a shelf and three pegs protruding from the wall over each bedspace.

These conditions, basic as they were, marked a real improvement on those which had prevailed in barracks of the eighteenth and early nineteenth centuries. No trace of these buildings remains in Britain today; but in Canada eighteenth-century army posts once occupied by British regiments have been lovingly and accurately recreated in places like the Citadel in Halifax, Nova Scotia, Fort York in Toronto, and Old Fort George in Ontario near to the US-Canadian border. To visit them today is to see something of what barrack life was like some two centuries ago. Conditions for other ranks were indeed crowded and far from comfortable, but they should be seen within the context of a period in history when standards of personal comfort for the working class were generally low, so that soldiers with a roof over their heads and regular meals were not, perhaps, so badly off as we might think.

A barrack room in the 1870s was described by J.E. Acland, whose *Through the Ranks to a Commission* (1881) is a minor classic of Victorian military life. His description is of especial interest because such quarters were in use in older garrison towns like Aldershot and Colchester until after the Second World War:

> The walls were whitewashed and the floor bare boards; there were tables in the centre, sufficient for all the occupants of the room to sit down at once, and wooden forms to correspond . . . As a rule there is a space of about three or four feet between the bedsteads, and a man next a window is generally best off.

When Lieutenant Colonel (later Lieutenant General) J.M. Grierson wrote in 1899 that 'the old barracks have been . . . replaced by new ones, and the British soldier is now in the enjoyment of accommodation, which is not inferior to that of any other army', he was probably right. Edgar Wallace, who served as a private at Maidstone Barracks in the early 1890s, described it as consisting of 'two-storey wooden hutments of great antiquity; there was a modern block consisting of four large rooms, two in each wing; hutments and brick block formed two sides of a square, which was bounded on the remaining two sides with one-storied married quarters.'

Barracks in use today reflect the much higher living standards of the time, and the old communal rooms in which twenty or more men lived are virtually a thing of the past. The improvements in the living conditions of soldiers which have taken place over recent years are a direct development of an enlightened building programme which produced much of the accommodation in Catterick Camp, Yorkshire, and establishments like Houndstone Barracks near Yeovil in Somerset, just before the outbreak of war in 1939. At that period the soldier's living-quarters varied: the old co-existed with the new. The fortunate ones lived in new buildings, built on the so-called 'spider' principle, a complex of huts linked to all facilities except the dining hall by corridors, and centrally heated. Today accommodation is of a uniformly high standard. Recruits occupy 'dormitories' which normally hold ten men, and sometimes as few as four trained soldiers will share one purpose-built room.

For soldiers living in barracks the working day, from beginning to end, was regulated by trumpet calls. (The trumpet came into use in the British army towards the end of the eighteenth century; before then the drum had been used for the 'beat to arms'.) There is, however, a considerable difference between the routine calls of the military day and the emotive fanfares which are so expertly played on occasions of public ceremony. Trumpet calls are no longer used to regulate troop movements in battle, but they are still used in barracks wherever possible, and the words that soldiers put to them are traditional.

First call of the day is reveille played, like most calls, at least twice. The unofficial words to it went like this:

> Get out of bed
> Get out of bed
> You lazy bugger
> I feel sorry for you
>   I do . . . oo.

Mealtimes were heralded with:

> Come to the cookhouse door, boys,
> Come to the cookhouse door.

Before first parade of the day 'Fall in' was sounded:

> Fall in "A"
> Fall in "B"
> Fall in every company.

Buglers, early nineteenth century.

A mounted drummer, early nineteenth century.

It is interesting to note that when the Duke of Wellington, as Colonel Arthur Wellesley, issued his Standing Orders in 1798 for the 33rd Regiment, he was very precise about the varied duties of each each company's Orderly Sergeant – and many of these are still his responsibility in the contemporary army. They would include a whole range of day-to-day matters relating to the efficient running of the unit. Round about mid-morning, orderly sergeants would be summoned to Regimental Headquarters with the following traditional call:

> A big duck shat in a little duck's eye.
> What did the little duck say?
> Shi . . . t (*a long drawn out note*).

The arrival of mail was announced with the following trumpet call:

> Letters from lousy Lizzie (*rising note*)
> Letters from lousy Lou (*falling note*).

Midday and the cookhouse call sounded again. After the day's parades, when most men were off duty, 'Defaulters' would be sounded: men who, for a variety of often trivial military 'crimes', had been sentenced to a period of C.B. (confined to barracks) of up to fourteen days would run ('double' in army parlance) to the Guard Room at the main entrance, where they were paraded, inspected, and then detailed for various unpleasant jobs ('fatigues'). The call went like this:

> You can do 'jankers' as long as you like
> As long as you answer the call . . .

Last call of the day was at about 10.30 p.m. This was tattoo or, in its shortest form:

> Lights out
> Lights out.

These are only some of the calls in use. There is a variation on reveille called 'The Arouse', which went like this:

> Charlie
> Charlie
> Get out of bed
> (*Repeat*).

Such calls were part of the daily routine for men in barracks, and are a far cry from Robert Graves's romanticised view of the trumpeter in England during the Great War sending out 'a call of high romance' when he played 'Lights out' on the darkened barrack square – I believe at Litherland Camp near Liverpool.

The history of trumpet calls is uncertain. Some of them may have been standardised by the reign of Henry VIII; some calls were played on the drum, but probably by the seventeenth century the trumpet was pre-eminent. It was a simple matter for a trumpeter on a horse to accompany a mounted officer, and orders could be conveyed while both were on the move. Moreover the trumpet note was more penetrating than the beat of a drum and could carry over a long distance even during battle. The one call which can be traced is tattoo, which was current in the army by 1644, coming into use when soldiers were quartered in private houses, and tattoo was the signal to landlords to stop serving drink, and to the troops to return to billets. The word itself derives from the Dutch 'doe den tap to', meaning turn off the taps or, in a slang form, 'shut up'.

To recreate the daily life of a soldier, over whatever period, is not an easy matter, and we have to establish at the outset some of the main differences between soldiering in war and in peace. Active service brings with it the possibility of being killed, wounded or taken prisoner: equally it can, for regulars, mean accelerated promotion and other kinds of advancement. Wartime also means an increase in the numbers serving, either as volunteers or as conscripts. As the army grows larger, so standards of accommodation and general living tend to fall, often quite considerably, and the older conventions of discipline become harder to enforce. Further, as was evident at the end of both the major wars of the twentieth century, because conscription had brought into the ranks of the army men who were not so ready to accept military service and all that it entailed once hostilities were over, there were disturbances amongst other ranks caused by grievances connected with demobilisation. The unrest in the army in 1919 and again in the mid-1940s is not relevant to this narrative except to the extent that it illustrates in a dramatic way the difference between a wartime army, which saw its duty as being done when the enemy was defeated, and a regular force which was ready and anxious for a return to 'real soldiering'. By this phrase was meant spit and polish, daily parades, kit inspections, the orderly rotation of units between military stations, and a settled – if dull – existence in some garrison at home or abroad.

Even so, there was an ambivalence amongst some regular soldiers in their attitudes to 'real soldiering'. Establishments would be reduced; there would be fewer battalions; not only were chances for promotion restricted, but for many, reduction in rank became an actuality – in some cases after the 1914–1918 war regular soldiers who had been granted temporary commissions were reduced to the ranks in the peace-time army. In earlier times after a war, the officers whose services were no longer required would go on the half-pay list, hoping that in a future conflict they would be recalled to active service and the full pay of their rank.

Such changes in fortune, however, were rarely of pressing concern to men in the ranks who had chosen the profession of arms. For those at the bottom of the military hierarchy, the great watershed in their lives was passing from the status of raw recruit to that of trained soldier. Today when a young man joins the infantry his training takes nineteen weeks, at the end of which period it is just possible that he could find himself on active duty in the streets of Belfast. It has not always taken so long. Roger Lamb, for example, who was to become a sergeant in the 23rd Foot, tells us in his *Memoir of His Own Life* (1811) that he was drilled four hours a day for twenty-one days, after which he was issued with a musket and began his instruction in the manual exercise – what is now referred to as arms drill. 'The most disagreeable days of a soldier', he wrote, 'are those in which he begins his exercise.' He also characterises the old drill sergeants as unnecessarily severe. William Cobbett, on the other hand, who joined the 54th Foot in 1784, complained about exercising with a musket, when a recruit, for six to eight hours every day. The life of a recruit has remained hard right down to the present time. It has been characterised by an officer involved in it as tough but fair, to be regarded as a period of self-discovery, growing confidence and mental stamina, and the development of self-discipline and organisation. No drill sergeant at any time could have encapsulated so well the ideas underlying the making of new soldiers. This includes the cavalry, who had a different regime. After learning how to march and perform basic footdrill they were trained in the use of comb, sponge and brush; how to feed and water a horse; how to clean out the stables; saddling, unsaddling, and how to ride. Today in the various technical corps of the army training, after basic drill, becomes increasingly specialised.

Before training, of course, there is the issue of uniform and equipment. According to legend the army has only two official sizes: 'too large' and 'too small'. Today it officially recognises three sizes: small, medium and large – but uniforms are modified where necessary to fit individual

A soldier in Egypt having his hair cut, 1882. Traditionally, soldiers' hair had been grown to the length of one foot, then turned up in a single roll called a 'club', which was greased, powdered and held in position by a leather strap; in some units this was decorated with a regimental emblem. In about 1808 it was ordered that hair should be worn short. In the 23rd Foot, and probably in other regiments, the order was much resented, particularly by wives who took great pride in dressing their husbands' hair. It soon became apparent that short hair was clean, convenient and comfortable.

soldiers. It is the wearing of uniform which sets the army physically apart from the society of which it is so important an articulation, and it was in the period from 1680 to 1720 that national unity in military dress was very largely achieved. According to Sir George Clark in *The Seventeenth Century* (1950):

> Uniforms for the common soldier were introduced into England in the New Model Army of the Civil War; in France by degrees in the reign of Louis XIV. There were examples of them in the sixteenth century, and some troops dressed according to their fancy even in the eighteenth; but the general European adoption of uniform was a seventeenth-century process. No one who has ever worn a uniform can doubt that it was a decisive step in the history of discipline.

Closely connected with the rise of uniform, there was an increasing standardisation of army practices and procedures. Regulations, punishments and other paraphernalia of military discipline were developing over the same period, and there was, quite perceptibly, the beginnings of an administrative literature concerned not with the tactical handling of troops in battle, but rather with the day-to-day running of a regiment. It was this development from about the middle of the eighteenth century which argues strongly for an increasingly professional approach by many regimental officers to the task of ensuring that the units in which they served ran efficiently.

So far as uniforms were concerned, red coats were the commonest wear amongst infantry and cavalry. Specialist corps often favoured other colours – the artillery, for example, wore blue coats with red facings. Coloured uniforms were in vogue until the end of the nineteenth century. It was following the disaster at Majuba Hill in 1881, when red-coated soldiers, their uniforms offering an easy target against the background of the South African veld, were decimated by Boer sharp-shooters, that khaki uniforms were introduced into the Indian Army in 1885. They were universally worn by British troops during the Second South African War, and by 1902 khaki was a standard issue throughout the army. Scarlet uniforms survive in the Brigade of Guards, where they are still worn for ceremonial parades and for guard duties in London. Military bands, too, wear scarlet and other colours on special parades.

Issue of clothing and necessaries has become a time-honoured ritual in the army, and the RQMS (Regimental Quartermaster Sergeant) who presides in today's army over the kit parade – usually held on the first day of training – is the most recent in a long line of men who have carried out a similar function over several centuries. The RQMS in the contemporary army issues new recruits with clothing and other necessaries worth about £450, a sum which, even allowing for inflation, compares oddly with the £3 or so allowed to a colonel for clothing his regiment in the early eighteenth century, and reflects, of course, the increased complexity of a soldier's needs in the late twentieth century.

Uniforms, though, were not always treated with the respect that we might have thought. In the field on active service all kinds of modification, both official and unofficial, might be made. In 1758 during the Seven

RIGHT:
Regimental Quartermaster Sergeant (R.Q.M.S.) making certain that the cap of the man joining the Royal Artillery fits correctly. The picture dates from 1939 and the soldier receiving his initial issue of kit is an early conscript or 'militiaman', as they were called at this period.

PREVIOUS PAGE:
A private of the West Yorkshire militia, 1814. The militia was raised on a county basis to assist the regular army in defence of the country: its members were not called upon to serve abroad unless they volunteered to do so. It was in many respects the forerunner of the Territorial Army (founded 1921), sometimes derisively and unfairly referred to as 'Saturday-night soldiers', and the contemporary Volunteer Reserves. Note that this soldier is wearing spatterdashes or leggings, which served both to prevent stones and grit from working their way into his shoes, and to keep his legs dry.

Years War the following anonymous item, relating to the British army in Massachusetts, was printed in *The Boston News-Letter* dated 6 July:

> You would laugh to see the droll Figure we all cut; Regulars and Provincials are all ordered to cut the Brims of their Hats off: The following is General Abercromby's Orders; That no Person, Officer or Private, be allowed to carry more than one Blanket and a Bearskin, no Sash nor Sword, nor even Lace to be worn upon Guard, a small Portmanteau to be allowed each Officer; even the General himself is allowed to carry no more than a common private's Tent. The Regulars as well as the Provincials have left off their proper Regimentals, that is, they have cut their Coats so as scarcely to reach their Waist: You would not distinguish us from common Ploughmen: – No Women to follow the Camp, to wash our Linen; Lord Howe, who is second in Command, has already shewed an Example, by going himself to the Brook, and washing his own Linen: When we go from Fort Edward every Officer is to carry his own Pack, Provisions, etc., no Horses being allowed us.

Soldiers stationed in Halifax, Nova Scotia, in 1848–1849 were issued with special winter clothing which was made in the province. One pound ten shillings (£1.50) per man was set aside for expenditure on certain garments which were expected to last the wearer for prescribed periods of time: a fur cap, for example, had to last for three years, Canadian boots for at least two. Orders setting out the relevant regulations stressed the need for uniformity in the manufacture of such clothing. It should be mentioned, too, that after an initial issue, soldiers would be expected to pay for all repairs and untoward replacements.

During the Great War men in the trenches wore a variety of clothes to protect themselves against the cold and wet weather in France and Flanders. There would be greatcoats, for example, from which the sleeves had been cut in order to give greater ease in handling rifles and Lewis-guns. Sheepskin jerkins were also worn, together with Balaclava helmets knitted by family and friends at home. The problem of keeping men's feet dry in the trenches was never satisfactorily solved. In heavy rain and mud, boots and puttees speedily became waterlogged.

There is a story told about Field Marshal Lord Montgomery when he was commanding the 8th Army in the Western Desert. Travelling in an open staff car, he met a three-ton truck travelling in the opposite direction whose driver, naked from the waist, was wearing an elegant top hat that he had apparently come upon in his travels. Montgomery could not be avoided, so the driver of the truck, with great aplomb, acknowledged the Army Commander by elegantly raising his headgear. Montgomery returned a smart salute and the two vehicles went their separate ways. A few days later there appeared in Army Orders a directive to the effect that top hats would not be worn in the 8th Army! This was apparently the only clothing regulation that Montgomery issued in the desert.

Finally so far as clothing is concerned, there is a grim reminder in the Public Archives of Canada (RG8 Vol. 344 p.68) of the uniform worn by military convicts who were held on St Helen's Island near Montreal. A clothing order for the year 1846 included: '100 Great Coats of Canadian Grey Cloth, with red facings, seams and Breast, 200 pairs of thick flannel drawers, 100 pairs of long moccasins, 100 pairs of mittens and 100 fur caps'. Grey uniforms faced with red were laid down in military prison regulations issued in 1847, but documentation on army convicts and army prisons in the nineteenth century is extremely sparse.

About other matters of military discipline much more is known. The uniform that soldiers wore set them apart from society in a way that all could see. Much less obvious to society at large, though not to the soldier himself, was the fact that he lived his life under military law. Such law was first laid down in the Articles of War, one of the earliest complete sets of which was published at Newcastle in 1639 under the title *Laws and Ordinances of Warre, for the better Government of his Majesties Armie Royall, in the present Expedition for the Northern Parts . . . etc.* The document falls into two parts, the first dealing with blasphemy, swearing, cursing, robbing churches and attendance at divine service. Gambling was singled out for special mention and was prohibited 'for as much as gaming is oft times the provocation into swearing, quarrelling, neglect of moral duties, with the dishonour of God Almightie, loss to the souldiers with danger to the whole army'. It was also laid down that 'suspitious and common women' were to be turned out of camp, and if they returned were to be 'soundly whipped like common strumpets'. Death was prescribed for several offences including murder, rape, setting fire to houses, theft outrage, unnatural abuses, 'notorious and abominable crimes'. The first section concluded with this requirements: 'No enterprise shall be taken in hand, but the company that are to execute the same shall first commend themselves to God and pray to Him to grant them good success.'

The second part opens with a general warning about treachery, which includes any disparagement of the high command. Anyone who spoke against its 'actions or directions . . . unlesse he be able to make it good,

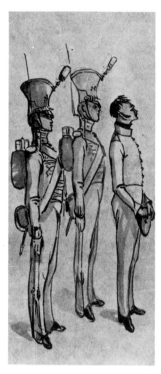

A defaulter, early nineteenth century. For infringements of military discipline, the accused soldier had to make an appearance – hatless, unless he were a non-commissioned officer – before his company or battery commander, who was empowered to deal with non-serious offences. Where matters were more serious, the soldier would be remanded to appear before (OPPOSITE) the regimental commanding officer, whose powers were wider and who could, in very serious cases, remand for a court martial.

shall die for it'. Then there were regulations regarding assaults on officers and consumption of rations or ammunition in less than the prescribed period for which they were issued. Camp sanitation was mentioned, and there was concern with the burning of 'garbage, carrion, filth and other noysome offences', a duty which was the responsibility of the Provost Marshal. Regulations against pillaging and the intimidation of civilians were set out. Any offence not specifically mentioned would be dealt with according to what was called the 'ancient course of marshall discipline', and there was further provision for the collective punishment of regiments deemed guilty of an offence. The Articles of War made up a comprehensive document which was much amended and extended over the years. If these rules – and today there is a substantial body of military law – have laid down in unambiguous terms through the years just what a soldier may or may not do, then it seems reasonable to ask how things worked out in practice during his (and in the present century, her) daily life. No problem of legal theory is at issue here: we need to know how the fabric of routine, with its pattern of hierarchy, was kept from unravelling.

There was scarcely any aspect of a soldier's life that was not subject to regulation, and an over-zealous officer, sergeant-major or sergeant could make the life of a man in the ranks a misery. With a degree of mutual respect, tolerance, fairness and even sensitivity, even under the most desperate circumstances – after the Third Battle of Ypres in 1917, for instance – the army did for the most part hang together. Soldiers who were perpetually aggrieved, or who saw themselves as the objects of a brutal and repressive discipline, would not have acquitted themselves in the field, whether in victory or defeat, so well as the British army has traditionally done. When the system broke down, as it nearly did in Étaples in 1917, or during 1919 when demobilisation processes were perceived by many soliders to be unfair, those in authority were on the whole responsible. Where there were mutinies of Indian or African troops – and these did not occur often – they have nearly always been caused by attitudes of racial superiority and an insensitivity to the feelings of men under their command on the part of white officers. By no means all were guilty of such stupidity, but because of the few who were, the army occasionally paid a high price in mistrust and in dissipated loyalty. The problem has always been one of strking a balance. In the eighteenth century an almost grotesque failure on the part of the government to grasp the strength of Scottish feeling provoked mutiny in several Scots regiments, and in the nineteenth there was often a problem with Irish soldiers. The fact remains, however, that the balance has in general been fairly struck, and the army has run well.

Mutiny apart, the most serious of military offences were probably desertion, striking a superior officer or being asleep while on sentry duty. Amongst others very much less serious were drunkenness, loss of kit, petty pilfering, overstaying furlough ('absence without leave' was a much lesser crime than desertion), being late on parade, dirty bedspace, being unshaven on parade – and these were only some of the offences a man might commit. The most curious was that of 'dumb insolence', which might imply no more than that a soldier did not look submissive when reproved by a superior in rank, but it was regarded as seriously as 'answering back'. (This offence was done away with just before or during 1939.) For any of these and other 'crimes' a soldier might be charged with 'Conduct to the prejudice of good order and military discipline'. Many offences were trivial, and treated as such. Oaths and blows were commonplace in an age when flogging was a customary punishment for defaulters . . . and Corporals of Horse in Cromwell's army, sergeants in Marlborough's, and their successors until well into the nineteenth century would have had recourse to such methods.

Lieutenant-Colonel John Blackader, who served in the armies of William III and the Duke of Marlborough, 'made some severe examples of punishment' when faced with problems of 'cursing, swearing, drunkenness, robbing, thieving, mutiny, etc.' amongst his men, but he did not go into details about either the crimes or the specific punishments. It is probably safe to assume that his problems were not untypical, though he may have allowed his irritation to run away with his pen, and it is difficult to know exactly what he meant by 'mutiny'. It seems likely from the context that it was insubordination rather than the much more serious crime, but we cannot be sure.

The fortunate survival of a slim MS volume in the Kent Archives Office, containing details of courts martial conducted in the army of Sir William Waller in 1644, enables us to know something of the ways in which serious infringements of discipline were dealt with at this period. John Boreman, 'a foote soldier', was accused of 'makeing a Mutiny . . . and then running away'. He was apprehended, and after a court martial at which five witnesses were called, he was sentenced to be hanged. The trial seems to have been a fair one and civilian witnesses were summoned by warrant to testify before the court. Trooper Henry Wilcocke faced charges of robbing Thomas Collier, a miller, who was also served with a warrant ordering him 'to appear at the next Councell of War to give testimony against the abovesayd Henry Wilcocke, and another Trooper for Robbing of him'. Wilcockc's fate is uncertain, but another soldier, John Whitaker, arraigned for highway robbery in Dorset, was sentenced to be hanged. A lesser punishment was awarded to 'Corpall Vandradisse', who absented himself from guard duty. He was sentenced to 'ride the woo
dden horse according to discrecon'. This was a lighter punishment often employed for minor offences. For a given period the culprit sat astride the wooden horse, which was made of two boards nailed together to make a sharp ridge or angle, with four posts forming the legs. The feet of the man so punished would be weighted with muskets. Richard Allen, a regimental surgeon attached to the train of artillery, stood trial for neglecting his duty, disobeying the orders of Dr Pratt, Physician of the Army, and 'abusing him with abusive and contemptuous language'. The case revolved round the treatment of an injured man, and witnesses stated that Allen had called Pratt a 'foole, asse and Coxcombe' after a dispute about treatment and blood letting. Allen was sentenced to be cashiered, and to imprisonment until the 'next Councell of Warr, and this to stand in force

until the further will and pleasure of the Generall be known'. There is no record of Allen's subsequent fate.

At Stow on the Wold, Sergeant West of Waller's Regiment of Foot was accused of abusing men in the Tower Hamlets Regiment, and had to apologise in public. As the record says: 'It is ordered that Sergeant West for that he by his own confession abused in some scandalous and reproachful language the Hamblets souldiers that he stand Comitted until their forces be drawne up, and that then hee shall in the head of the Regiment make an humble acknowledgement of his fault'. There was a general sanction in Waller's Army against drunkenness, and the Provost Marshal was authorised 'so often he shall finde any private Souldier drunke, that hee shall have the power to inflict the punishment of putting on a paire of handcuffs, and with a chaine to draw the party up untill hee stands on tiptoe, with a Kan or jugg about his necke neer the maine Guard, and there to stand according to discrecon.' Towards the end of 1644 there was concern about soldiers plundering civilians, and the death penalty was threatened for such offences. Sometimes officers were court martialled. Major Willett, found guilty of falsifying muster returns, was cashiered; but Captain Potter, accused of killing one of his men, Trooper Mathew White, was acquitted because the dead man had been a trouble-maker.

During the eighteenth century, army discipline was often characterised by a brutality that was endemic in society at large. Things had been similar in the seventeenth century, and the age of enlightenment brought little change. So much in the society of the time helped to breed callousness and an acceptance of human suffering: public hangings, whipping at the cart's tail, the pillory, appalling prison conditions, the exploitation of lunatics confined in bedlam as an entertainment for visitors, cruelty to animals – bull-running and bear-baiting are examples – together with the degradations of poverty, drunkenness and much gratuitous violence. On all of this the efforts of reformers like John Howard could make, initially, but little impression.

It should be said that a considerable majority of serving men accepted the disciplinary conventions of the army without question, and were not wrongdoers caught up in the web of violent punishment which entrapped the deserter or the confirmed 'bad bargain' in the ranks. Most men did their jobs without being flogged and did not desert, choosing rather to soldier on with the dogged resilience that they so often displayed in battle, notwithstanding a tendency to swear and grumble amongst themselves. In the eighteenth century, for the first time, the British army was scattered throughout the world as imperial conquests made increasing demands upon infantry battalions called upon both to fight for and then to occupy the lands that they won. At the same time troops stationed at home tended to be split up into detachments assisting the civil power in actions against smuggling and riot, and only rarely came together as regimental units. Despite these different demands made on it, and despite the violence of the times, the army did remain a coherent and flexible arm of the state. As it has been suggested earlier, had the men in the ranks been crushed by too

OPPOSITE:
William Cobbett served in the ranks for eight years, having, he wrote 'passed through every rank, from that of private sentinel to that of Sergeant-Major, without ever once being disgraced, confined or even reprimanded.' His reason for leaving the service was disgust at the peculation by which a quarter of the men's provisions were retained for the private use of the Quartermaster. Cobbett's accusations led to this court-martial at Portsmouth in 1792, but political pressures thwarted his aims, and Cobbett absented himself from the court. His account of this sorry episode (to be found in *The Progress of a Plough-Boy to a Seat in Parliament*) shows how difficult it was for 'other ranks' to substantiate any complaint against their superiors.

repressive a discipline they would not have carried out so consistently well the many tasks imposed upon them. Of course men did desert, there were major infringements of discipline, there were floggings and military executions; but these things did not occur on such a scale as to make them anything but exceptional happenings.

It seems that commanding officers were probably more exercised in their minds by slack discipline such as not turning up for roll-call. General Orders issued by Lord Loudoun in North America in 1757 indicate some of the more usual concerns: 'As Some Persons Have Hitherto Contrary to Orders Indulged them Selves in Not Turning out at Roll Calls – For ye Future they who Don't Appear at the Place Appointed as Soon as ye Drum has Done Beating Are to be Confind and tried by a Coort Martial.' This was dated 18 May, and the same orders included a warning to 'Connecticutt Troops' who were thought to be deficient of the ammunition that had been issued to them. The document stated that they 'May Expect to be delt with as Embezzlers of ye Kings Stores'. A few months later, in August, there was another warning that anyone found 'Stealing Plank or timber belonging to ye Kings works will be Sevearly Punish.d Emediately – and ye Persons to whom ye huts belong will be Responsible for it if any Such Timber is found in them.'

If such items in General Orders made up the stuff of daily routine in the army at home or abroad, there is no doubt that it was the more serious crimes which caught the public eye. Between July and December 1752 there was a series of reports in *The Worcester Journal* regarding a deserter from the 2nd The Queen's Dragoon Guards who turned out to be a Jacobite who had enlisted after the rebellion of 1745 had been put down. The man concerned, Thomas Anderson, was arrested in Perth, not as a runaway soldier but as a 'Gentleman and his Servant' who went under the names of Charles Douglas and Thomas Jones and 'could give no satisfactory Account of themselves'. The servant was soon released, but Anderson, alias Douglas (Milbank and Sympson were other pseudonyms) remained in custody 'on Suspicion of seditious Practices', and after further enquiry it was established that he was a deserter from the army. He was remanded for a court martial. The story rumbled on in the paper, and it emerged that a charge of 'treasonable Practices' might be added to that of desertion. He was sent, under guard, from Scotland to Shrewsbury where the Dragoons were quartered, and his trial began towards the end of November. Although he was eventually charged only with desertion, the paper remarked that 'there never was so long and remarkable Trial of a Person for Desertion only . . .' Anderson was found guilty and sentenced to be shot, a sentence which was carried out on 14 December 1752. With its undertones of espionage – Anderson was something of a linguist and had travelled extensively in Europe – the case attracted a good deal of local attention and the details of his death were published in full. At the place of execution he 'took a Handkerchief, and held it up in his Hand, and after praying privately for about five Minutes, dropp'd the Handkerchief as a Signal for the Soldiers to fire, which three of them immediately did; and three more were ready to have fir'd in case there had been occasion.'

This description of a military execution seems remarkably accurate if we compare it with the Directions for Execution Parties which were current in 1763:

The soldiers pitched upon for this disagreeable duty must be sober, cool, and steady men. They are to be formed into a small party, and commanded by a good sergeant, who is to carefully examine their firelocks, and see they are well loaded, and have good flints in them. He is to give the men a clear idea of what they are to perform, beforehand, that no mistakes may be committed.

The party being ordered to attend, stands shouldered, till the prisoner has finished his devotions, upon which the sergeant moves his hand, and the party 'makes ready', without the least noise; when the prisoner makes a signal, which is always done, the party immediately 'present' silently, without planting their feet, levelling directly at his breast, the moment they have presented, the sergeant moves his hand again, upon which the men instantly fire.

There must be a body of reserve in the rear, with their firelocks cocked, ready to fire if the first does not take place.

I have quoted these regulations at some length because, taken together with the newspaper report of an actual execution, they enable us to see something of the way in which written regulations worked out in practice. We are offered a rare insight, too, into the considerations which would have been present in a regimental officer's mind when he had to choose a firing party to carry out what was truly a 'disagreeable duty'. The grisly process of execution finds an echo in Rudyard Kipling's poem 'Danny Deever', which describes another military execution towards the end of the nineteenth century.

The whole subject of discipline is shown in its most repellent aspect when we consider attempts made in the nineteenth century to abolish flogging in the army. It was a time-honoured ritual punishment, carried out in front of the victim's fellow soldiers in order to impress them with the consequences of offending against military law. In earlier times, when the use of physical violence was both widespread and rarely questioned, few voices were raised against it. Daniel Defoe, it is true, did question the practice as early as 1722. Writing as 'A Corporal', though he never served in the army, he argued thus:

An honourable Punishment a Soldier never declines; such as running the Gauntlet, as it was call'd, which, tho' it be a Lash, yet there is something Masculine in it; but to be Tortur'd, tied Hand and Foot to a Post; to be whipt like a Rascal, or a Thief, or a Pick-Pocket, it makes a Gentleman abhor the very Cloth he wears, and refuse to show his Face any more; or, in Revenge, or go over to the Enemy . . .

Defoe's remained a lone voice for something like one hundred years. Efforts to change army procedures and disciplinary codes have to be seen against the background of modernising traditional British institutions which went on during the Age of Reform. The leaders of the army at the Horse Guards in London remained contemptuously and arrogantly opposed to any change, and flogging was defended as the most effective way of maintaining discipline. During the Napoleonic Wars the young Palmerston was convinced that corporal punishment 'was essential to the very existence of the Army'. Later in the century Field Marshal Viscount Wolseley wrote that it was 'cheap, simple, and withdrew the soldier from his duty for the shortest possible time'. Such views were increasingly at variance with the changing moral climate of the nineteenth century, but it was not until 1881 that flogging was finally abolished. It is worth noting, too, that the branding of deserters and 'bad characters' – a practice justified by the authorities as preventing multiple enlistments and protecting the public – had been abolished ten years earlier in 1871.

Debates in the House of Commons which touched on matters of military discipline were remarkable mainly for their demonstration of entrenched class attitudes and for the fallacious arguments resorted to by Parliamentary Colonels who, to a man, argued that the lash was essential to the efficient running of the army. Why, *The Times* asked in 1864, could the army not attract to its ranks the kind of man who will not require to be flogged? The question went unanswered, but eventually public opinion and the threat of falling enlistment figures forced a change. Corporal punishment was reduced to a maximum of twenty-five lashes (over five thousand had been inflicted upon one man some years earlier) in 1879, and it was abolished completely two years later. Change in public opinion had been brought about largely by the press, including *The Lancet*, a professional medical journal which took a strong line against flogging. There was even a ballad hawked about the streets entitled 'Never Flog Our Soldiers'. One serving officer spoke out strongly: he was Colonel William Jebb, Director of Military Prisons in the late 1850s, and he argued forthrightly against the use of the cat-of-nine-tails, claiming that if barrack accommodation were better 'the less will be the crime and the higher will be the character of the Army.'

Two soldiers who had known what life in the ranks was like made notable contributions to the debate. One of them was Staff Sergeant John Teesdale of the Royal Military College, Sandhurst, who had served for many years in the 28th Foot. In 1835 he published a longish pamphlet entitled *Military Torture – a Letter Addressed to the People of England on the Use of the Cat o' Nine Tails in the British Army*. The author does not spare the feelings of his readers: he describes the gory ceremony of flogging and gives specific examples. Sir Thomas Picton had three of his men lashed on the field of Waterloo, one of whom was killed by enemy fire two hours later. Teesdale describes the feelings of the drummer boys who (in infantry regiments) carried out the beating with 'no possibility of shrinking without the certainty of a rattan over the shoulders', and writes of the sense of degradation felt by flogger, victim and spectator alike. His polemic and convincing argument is confirmed in a number of the rank and file memoirs published in the first half of the nineteenth century. The other was an 'Army Veteran' who wrote to Charles Dickens' magazine *All the Year Round* in 1865: 'I am not only quite sure that no soldier was ever reformed by the lash, but no bad man ever became good after being flogged.'

Official opposition to the abolition of corporal punishment shows successive government ministers, a majority of senior officers and many junior ones in a very poor light. Their attitudes ensured that until the end of the nineteenth century the British Army remained saturated in the

traditions of an earlier age, and failed in almost every way to show any awareness of the profound social changes which were beginning to ameliorate the conditions of the working classes. Behind the public parades, cheering crowds, bands, scarlet jackets, gold braid and pipeclay – the image of the Victorian army that has come down to us – there lurked a mean reality long hidden from posterity.

With the eventual abolition of flogging, and with other reforms, life in the ranks became significantly better. Discipline remained strict, and while the death penalty and long prison sentences were the ultimate sanctions for recalcitrant soldiers, in the case of lesser breaches of discipline, punishments meant periods of confinement to barracks, other curtailments of personal liberty, fatigue duties and forfeiture of pay – all of which continue to the present time.

There was a clear distinction between confinement in the cells of a regimental guard room and committal, for serious offences, to a military or a civil prison. This might be preceded by the ancient ceremony of 'Drumming Out', two cases of which were reported in *The Times* during 1863. On 18 May it described the scene at Colchester three days earlier:

Military flogging, early nineteenth century. The victim is closely observed by the regimental surgeon (in a dark coat) and, to his left, the sergeant-major of the regiment keeps a tally of the strokes inflicted, the drummers tapping a single beat every time the lash falls. The commanding officer and his adjutant, both mounted, are seen to the right. One soldier in the unit, which has been paraded to watch the grisly spectacle, has been overcome by the sight and fainted.

On Friday a private named Smith, of the 5th Fusiliers, was drummed out of his regiment. Smith had been for some time in hospital for treatment of rigidity of the knee. The medical officers, believing that his lameness was feigned, administered chloroform, and the knee was instantly bent. He was tried by court martial and sentenced to be expelled the army, and to undergo six months imprisonment. About noon on Friday the 10th battalion was mustered near the Military Hospital, and Smith was brought, with other prisoners from the guardhouse. The sentence upon the culprit was read aloud and he was stripped of his buttons, facings, etc. The battalion then formed a line on either side of the roadway, and, preceded by a corporal and private, and led by a rope attached to his neck by the smallest drummed boy, Smith marched to the gate, the band playing 'The Rogue's March'. On leaving the gate he was supplied with an overcoat, and was taken in charge by an escort, which accompanied him to Coldbath-fields Prison, where he will undergo the six months hard labour. During the whole of these proceedings Smith inflexibly maintained his composure, and persisted in his pretence that he is lame.

On 9 November there was another report:

On Friday, in accordance with the sentence of a court martial, the ceremony of 'drumming out' a soldier was performed at Aldershott [sic]. The culprit was Private Peter O'Donnell, of the 76th Regiment, whose extraordinary attempt at desertion was noticed in *The Times* about three months ago. It will be remembered that O'Donnell escaped, with his rifle, bayonet, and 20 rounds of ammunition in his possession, into the Long Valley, and for three days kept a pursuing party at bay, being ultimately lost sight of in the direction of Reading. Subsequently he quietly returned to his regiment, was placed under arrest, and tried by court martial for the offence. Being found guilty on several counts of desertion, firing at a corporal of the 76th Regiment and a private of the 6th Dragoon Guards, and of losing various articles of regimental apparel, ammunition, etc., he was adjudged to undergo 'four years penal servitude, to be ignominiously expelled Her Majesty's service, and to be branded with the letter "D".' The two companies of the 76th Regiment remaining at Aldershott having assembled in the barrack square, together with the band of the 60th Rifles, the prisoner was marched out handcuffed, wearing only his shirt and trousers, as when last seen at the period of his escape. Since his arrest he has constantly feigned insanity, and he now exhibited a very defiant bearing. The companies being drawn into line, and the front rank marched 15 paces to the front, Captain O'Donaghue, the senior officer in command, read the charge and the finding of the court martial, together with the whole list of offences recorded against the prisoner, from which it appeared that his name had figured in the defaulters' book 41 times, and that he had previously, at Glasgow, been sentenced to 112 days' imprisonment, and to be branded with the letter "D". On the conclusion of the reading of the sentence the prisoner threw his cap high in the air, and shouted 'Long Live Queen Victoria! Good bye! Three cheers for old Ireland!!'. Quickly stepping out, he was followed by the band of the 60th Rifles playing 'The Rogue's March'. On arriving at the end of the line he turned round, bowed nearly to the ground, again shouted 'Good bye!' and threw his cap into the air two or three times. He was then marched, under an escort of the 60th Rifles, to the military prison to undergo his full term of punishment.

Some elements in the ceremony are common to both accounts: reading the sentence, playing the 'Rogue's March' and marching the prisoner out of barracks. There are some differences between the two, and it would be interesting to know the precise extent to which tradition dictated separate regimental practices on such occasions. Even more interesting in the Aldershot drumming out is the detailed description of O'Donnell's offences. Presumably he was one of the Queen's 'bad bargains'.

So far as a soldier's life in prison is concerned, we have very little to go on. Few men wrote about the experience, but an oblique light is thrown upon regimental imprisonment in a brief note published in the *United Service Journal* in May 1836:

> In 1819, there being no cells attached to the barracks allotted to the Infantry Regiment in garrison at Portsmouth, a man under sentence was sent to Southsea Castle, and confined in a small place under the bomb-proof, with a hole in the rampart above to let in air, which in rainy weather was closed with a plug. To admit air in bad weather, he was allowed to thrust a wisp of straw between the thin yielding door and the jamb, until a hole was cut in the floor, and then it required two sentries, one above and one below, to prevent meat and liquid being carried to him, with the chance of one of the sentries being his dissolute comrade.

The prisoner in this piece is anonymous, but the hint of illicit camaraderie is fascinating.

Edgar Wallace was far from anonymous, and when he was a soldier during the 1890s he served a short sentence in a military prison. He described the experience in his autobiography, and it is the only account of a military imprisonment that I have found. Wallace had walked out of his barracks in Aldershot and spent five unauthorised days in London celebrating the performance in public of a music-hall song that he had written. On his return he was charged with being absent without leave and taken before his commanding officer. The sentence was prison with hard labour for ninety-six hours (known in the army as 'half a packet', a 'full packet' being one hundred and sixty-eight hours). Private Wallace was then marched by Sergeant Ben Hannan to the military prison in Aldershot, usually known as the 'glass house', where discipline can only be described as ferocious. His head was shaved, he was issued with convict dress ornamented with broad arrows, locked in a cell, fed upon skilly and potatoes and set to pick oakum. On the following day he paraded for shot drill, an agonising and humiliating punishment which was abolished in 1904. Wallace described it in these words:

> . . . I was marched out of the cell to a drill yard and initiated into the art of shot drill, the most damnable and heart-breaking punishment that was ever invented. You stand in four lines, a heavy iron shot at your feet. At the word of command you lift the shot breast high, turn left, march four paces and put it down. Walking back you find the shot that the man on your right has deposited. You lift this and follow the same routine, until you have carried four shots to the left. Then you carry them back again to the right.

Two days of this reduced Wallace to physical and mental exhaustion, and the prison chaplain intervened on his behalf so that the rest of his sentence was spent locked, solitary, in his cell, picking oakum. 'I was glad', wrote Wallace with great understatement, 'when my period of imprisonment was ended.' Painfully conscious of his shaved head, he returned to his unit, and there he was delighted to find that his fellow soldiers and superiors greeted him as though nothing untoward had happened and dismissed the whole incident that might easily have been experienced by anyone. It was a searing experience for Edgar Wallace, although he makes light of it in his autobiographical account.

For an army on active service when a formal declaration of war had been made, infringements of discipline could be dealt with by sentencing the offender to a period of Field Punishment Number One. The guilty soldier would be spreadeagled against the wheel of a wagon and tied to it by his wrists and ankles. This would be awarded for so many days, up to eight hours on the wheel constituting a day. Much used as a punishment in South Africa and on the Western Front, it was abolished by Lloyd George's government in 1916.

Confinement to barracks and extra fatigue duties speak for themselves. In the army today forfeiture of pay is often used, and in the winter of 1987 there was a ministerial investigation into the 'fines' awarded by the commanding officer of a unit stationed in Germany. One of his men forfeited eighteen days' pay for leaving his room in a filthy condition; another lost nineteen days' pay for riding a bicycle without lights and behaving in a disorderly manner. The officer was eventually cleared of allegations that he had intimidated and bullied his men, but more than a quarter of them had applied to be transferred to other units.

It is not easy to generalise about standards of discipline and their enforcement in the army today, for the army has enormous power over those who serve in it. Two stories will illustrate the range of possibilities. In 1942 the commanding officer of a driver training regiment stationed near Matlock in Derbyshire wished to curb what he perceived as a spreading slackness among the men in his unit. Accordingly he ordered that when salutes were exchanged between officers and men, the former would shout 'Hi de hi!' and the latter, springing to attention, would respond with 'Ho de ho!'. Inevitably the story found its way into the popular press, became a nine-day wonder . . . and the practice was speedily dropped. The unit left Matlock, its place being taken by a primary training unit whose discipline, despite the efforts of a venerable Rifle Brigade lieutenant colonel who commanded it, was much more relaxed. The other story comes from the Falkland Islands where, in the winter of 1987, a sergeant was court-martialled for striking an officer. This is a very serious offence, and the circumstances were unusual. There were, in fact, two trials. The officer – a lieutenant colonel – had struck the sergeant first!

Chapter 3

BARRACK LIFE

After becoming accustomed to the routine of barrack life and accepting the discipline which underlies it, the soldier very soon becomes aware of other factors which affect his daily round, and a major one is diet. Army food has traditionally been the object of criticism and derision – much of it unprintable. There is a cartoon by Bruce Bairnsfather of an old soldier during the Great War opening a tin of plum and apple jam, a standard issue on the Western Front. 'When the 'ell is it going to be strawberry?', he asks. The picture makes a telling point about the monotony of much army food and, by implication at least, reminds us that such a question could not possibly have been asked in earlier times when rations were much more limited in both variety and quantity.

Bread or biscuit and cheese seem to have been the staple items of food issued to troops in England and Scotland during the seventeenth century. Because men were so often quartered, willy nilly, with private house-holders and innkeepers, there was little incentive for the army to do more than make such basic food available. A glimpse of the ration issue can be gained from the account of a court martial which took place in Dundee in 1651. Two officers and a sergeant, in the upper room of a building, were supervising the issue of rations. The room was so crowded with expectant soldiers that the two officers attempted to clear some of them out. Ensign Kent ordered some of the men to leave, and Lieutenant Woodward shouted 'Get you out!' to one man who was pushing. As the man continued to shove Woodward hit him on the neck and thrust him downstairs, while the soldier shouted 'What, shall we not see our biscuit and cheese weighed, I hope to see such officers as you disbanded before long.'

The quantity of food issued is uncertain. During General Monck's 1654 campaign in the Scottish Highlands, it was customary for his infantry to carry a week's ration with them. This consisted of seven pounds of biscuit and probably three and a half pounds of cheese. On active service, rations could often be augmented by plunder or poaching. Despite ordinances issued by commanding officers against killing house pigeons, rabbits belonging to warrens, or breaking into houses, orchards and gardens, such practices went on. One soldier, Robert Bolter, stole a leg of mutton from a woman at Dundee. He was caught and sentenced to ride the wooden horse for an hour and to receive thirty lashes.

Cooking in the field was always a problem. It was not unknown for cavalry soldiers to use their back plates and helmets as cooking vessels: 'Some of our soldiers brought a little raw meat with them and became excellent cooks, a back makes a dripping-pan and a head-peece is a porrage pot', wrote one chronicler. What, one wonders, could the infantry, without such vestigial armour, have done?

A camp-follower tends the cooking-pot, early nineteenth century.

A sutler and her customers
in the Peninsula, 1803.

Despite the regulations regarding the unlawful seizure of provisions, there seems little doubt that during the Civil War both sides regarded 'enemy' sympathisers as fair game when it came to augmenting supplies. 'Every day', wrote Sergeant Nehemiah Wharton, an infantryman serving with the Parliamentary army in 1642, 'our soldiers by stealth do visit papists' houses, and constraine from them both meate and money. They give them whole great loaves and chesses, which they triumphantly carry away upon the points of their swords.' Later the same year Wharton mentions soldiers in the Midlands who entered Lord Dunsmore's park near Coventry and shot deer. They did this on a daily basis to such effect that for a time the consumption of venison was common amongst the rank and file of the city garrison. The army was not always so well fed. In September of the same year Wharton wrote: 'Our food was fruit, for those who could get it; our drink, water; our beds, the earth; our canopy, the clouds . . .' It seems clear that supplying a seventeenth-century army with food could be an irregular affair, and the key figure in it was the sutler, a civilian official whose emolument depended principally upon fees.

By the year 1702, when the Duke of Marlborough was beginning his campaigns in Flanders, we find the Commissariat – whose responsibilities covered pay, movement, all kinds of supplies including munitions on active service – issuing as provisions only bread. For all other food and drink troops were dependent upon sutlers. Each regiment had one grand sutler and each company or troop had a petty sutler. Their activities were regulated by the major of the regiment, who was responsible for seeing that they charged fair prices and sold by fair weight and measure, and that the goods offered for sale were fresh and wholesome. By chance the life story of a sutler with Marlborough's army has survived. The authorship is ascribed to Daniel Defoe, and the narrative was said to have been 'Taken from her own Mouth' when she was a pensioner at Chelsea Hospital. Mrs Christian Davies, commonly known as 'Mother Ross', was an Irishwoman whose lover had joined up when he was drunk. She too enlisted in another regiment, and fought in several engagements before her sex was discovered. On leaving the army she married her lover and stayed with him until his death at the Battle of Malplaquet in 1709. In order to support herself while she was married to a penniless soldier, she became a sutler, and she continued in this calling after she was widowed. According to her own account she catered for officers and for men very successfully and, despite Marlborough's strict orders against pillage and plunder, was not above stealing pigs, poultry and other items. As she put it, at the Siege of Douay 'I entered a chateau, deserted by the enemy, and found in it a basket of eggs, and another of cocks and hens (in the camp language, "corporals and their wives"), which I made free with . . . ' On another occasion she wrote: 'I got out of a barn a large bolster full of wheat, two pots of butter, and a great quantity of apples, all of which I carried safe to my tent. The wheat I got ground at a mill the enemy had deserted, and made pies which I sold in the camp . . . ' Clearly a person of great enterprise, she died years after the war in 1739, and was buried with military honours in the churchyard of St Margaret's, Westminster.

Being a sutler, providing food and drink under licence, could prove a very lucrative occupation. As Pistol in Shakespeare's *Henry V* put it: 'I shall sutler be/Unto the camp, and profits shall accrue.' But by the 1740s things were not quite so simple. There were increasing rules and regulations, one of which forbade any soldier or soldier's wife to apply for a sutler's licence. The extent to which this rule was enforced is problematic. In 1762 Samuel Hutton, serving with the 12th Foot in Germany, married the widow of a comrade who had been killed in action. 'She was a pretty little Scotchwoman . . . and got a great deal of money by keeping a suttling tent for officers . . . ' In Britain during the eighteenth century there were pretty well no sutlers at all in time of peace, for until the end of that century there were few purpose-built barracks where the trade could be plied. Troops were mainly on detachment – the six troops of a dragoon regiment, for example, might be quartered in as many small market towns – and they would be billeted at inns whose proprietors were required, under the provisions of the Mutiny Act, to provide such soldiers with food, fire and candle at a fixed tariff per man. In eighteenth-century Ireland, it is true, there were some barracks, and in them sutlers may have been active.

The question of feeding troops on foreign stations had arisen in the seventeenth century when there were garrisons in America and the West Indies. Their numbers, no less than the locations where they were stationed, grew during the eighteenth century. It was something of a shock for Members of Parliament to learn that in Gibraltar, Minorca and Nova Scotia there were no ale-houses where soldiers could be billeted, and that something exceptional would have to be done both for housing and for feeding the troops there. On foreign stations men were fed pretty generally as they would have been at sea, namely on salt meat but with bread instead of biscuit. An enlightened commanding officer would always augment such a diet with local vegetables and fruit in order to prevent outbreaks of scurvy and preserve the general health of his men.

The problems of feeding an army abroad do not come into a sharper focus until the American Revolution in 1775, when the garrison in the thirteen colonies and in Canada consisted of about 8,500 men. The coming of hostilities meant that reinforcements would be sent to North America, and, as their numbers grew, so too the problems of supplying them adequately became more acute. Since for most of the war British troops in America were confined within areas too small to provide adequate amounts of basic foodstuffs, and also because when local purchases could be made prices were inflated, provisions had to be sent out from home. The weekly ration of food for one man consisted of 7 lb. of bread or flour; 7 lb. of beef or 4 lb. of pork; 6 oz. of butter or 8 oz. of cheese; 3 pints of peas; 1/2 lb. of oatmeal. Throughout the war the demand for supplies fluctuated, 1781 being the peak year. The army never went hungry, despite the difficulties involved in feeding its soldiers more than 3,000 miles from their main source of supply. In practice, foodstuffs were divided for transit into two categories. Wet provisions comprised pork, beef and butter, the main source of which was Ireland. Dry provisions, which came mostly from England, consisted of flour, peas and oatmeal. The official diet of the army in America based upon the rations mentioned is easy enough to reconstruct. What is less certain is the extent to which the soldier's diet was augmented by small purchases of local food and drink, the high prices notwithstanding.

Amounts of food issued to troops on foreign stations showed slight variations. During the occupation of Madeira in 1801, for example, the daily ration comprised 1 lb. of bread; 10 1/3 oz. of meat; 1/6 quart of spirits; 1/7 quart of oatmeal; 3 oz. of peas. To avoid fractions in both issue and accounting, the allowance was calculated on the basis of six men for a week. In place of butter and cheese there was a weekly ration of one pint of molasses for six men, though it was pointed out that this was far short of the real value of butter and cheese.

All the food issued to men was paid for out of money stopped from their pay for this purpose. Troops at home received an issue of bread and meat, and there were traditionally two meals a day: breakfast at 7.30 and dinner at 12.30. This meant that the soldier was left for nineteen hours without food, a fact which, as we shall see, led ultimately to the establishment of wet and dry canteens in barracks. Towards the end of the nineteenth century, regimental cooks prepared meals for the men, and before the outbreak of the Great War in 1914 an Army School of Cookery had been established in Aldershot. The feeding of the men on the Western

Commissariat of the 3rd Division in the Crimea, 1855. Daily rations for men comprised 1 ½ lbs of bread or 1 lb of biscuit; 1 lb of fresh or salt meat; 2 oz of sugar; 1 oz of coffee or cocoa or ¼ oz of tea; 2 oz of rice; ½ oz of salt; ¼ oz of pepper for every eight men; 1 oz of lime juice; 1 gill of rum or porter in lieu at the rate of 2 quarts for every three men. Charcoal and wood for cooking were also supplied. In addition, 24,000 tons of forage per day were issued to the animals.

Front was a remarkable achievement. The British Expeditionary Force, unlike the troops sent to fight the Crimean War in the mid 1850s, never went hungry. If meals were rarely imaginative, they were almost always sufficient, and often prepared under the most trying conditions. The staple foods for men in the trenches were bully beef (similar to corned beef), biscuit, Tickler's plum and apple jam – made, so it was said, mostly from turnips – and tea, the latter nearly always made with heavily chlorinated water and sweetened with condensed milk. Biscuit constitutes one item in the twenty-four-hour three-meal ration pack used on exercises and active service today. It has been issued in one form or another – but always hard – since at least the seventeenth century, and so must surely be the most traditional of army foodstuffs.

Three meals a day had become customary before the end of the nineteenth century, although often 'tea' at four-thirty or five o'clock was a rather sketchy meal served by a cook who had probably been on duty all day and was anxious to finish . . . Field Marshal Robertson, who joined the 16th (Queen's) Lancers in 1877, described the food that he received while he was stationed in Aldershot:

> The food provided free consisted of one pound of bread and three-quarters of a pound of meat, and nothing more of any kind. Groceries, vegetables, and all other requirements were paid for by the men, who had a daily deduction of 3½d made from their pay of 1s.2d. for that purpose. The regulation meals were coffee and bread for breakfast; meat and potatoes for dinner, with soup or pudding once or twice a week; tea and bread for tea. If a man wished to have supper or something besides dry bread for breakfast and tea he had to purchase it from the barrack hawkers or canteen.

The way in which meals are taken in the army is normally defined by rank: private to corporal in a dining-hall; warrant officers/sergeants and officers in their separate messes. This picture is somewhat unusual as it shows men of various ranks in a Royal Electrical and Mechanical Engineers (R.E.M.E.) unit on active service in the Second World War, preparing food together. On the left a captain is frying some bacon; to the right a warrant officer class I holds a mess tin and mug. It is hard to imagine such free and easy attitudes being tolerated in, say, the Grenadier Guards, let alone photographed!

One of the most unforgettable and unpleasant rituals connected with rank and file eating during the Second World War, and probably earlier, was the washing up of one's own knife, fork, spoon and mug, which were part of a soldier's personal kit. This was carried out (and I refer to permanent camps in the United Kingdom, and not to units on active service where mess-tins were used) in baths of galvanised iron full of water, placed strategically at the exit doors of dining-halls. The water into which mug and 'eating irons' were dipped became progressively colder and greasier. There were no facilities for wiping the utensils, and the use of towels for this purpose was expressly forbidden. Conditions in this respect have improved.

Food during the Second World War was, so far as it is possible to judge, ample but dull. Soldiers fared, I think, rather better than civilians; but of course troops were at the mercy of those responsible for army feeding. During 1944 or thereabouts there was a campaign to persuade people in the British Isles to eat more potatoes, and in the camp in Derby where I was serving they were part of every meal for a period of time. On the other hand the army could take initiatives with food. One of the most successful concerned the humble sausage or 'banger' – 'barker' to an earlier generation of soldiers – which was consumed in large quantities. For some time after the defeat of Germany in 1945, the British Army of the Rhine was provided with them by a factory in Hanover which was run by military personnel.

The formation in March 1941 of the Army Catering Corps led eventually to a much more enlightened approach to food. The old 'beef and beer' tradition took a long time to die, and still flourished to some extent between 1914 and 1939. Since the war, army food has improved greatly and no longer enjoys the dreadful reputation that it once had. Choice of menu is readily available, and during the last few years, largely in response to the demands of women soldiers, non-fattening foods and health diets are to be had as a matter of course, if one wishes, in the larger garrison centres of Britain and Germany. So far as feeding is concerned the 'take it or leave it' attitude on the part of authority has changed. There is now a realisation that few things affect the morale and efficiency of the army more than food, and the Ministry of Defence seems to have come to terms both imaginatively and expertly with the requirements of today's serving soldiers.

For personnel in combat or on exercises simulating active service, provision is made in the form of the twenty-four-hour three-meal food pack to which reference has briefly been made. Since it has to be carried by a soldier who is already heavily loaded, both the shape of the pack and its weight are of importance. Considerable planning has gone into its composition, and the idea is to provide the user with about 4,500 calories, which should enable him to carry his pack and his weapons for a considerable distance on foot. The standard pack contains several items which include: steak and kidney pudding, bacon burgers, baked beans in three separate cans; rolled oats mix; beef stock; oxtail soup; processed cheese in a can; dried fruit mix; chocolate bar; boiled sweets; biscuit; fruit biscuit; tea bags; drinking chocolate; coffee powder; sugar; dried milk; dextrose tablets, orange flavour; salt; lemon powder; matches and toilet paper. Similar ration packs for groups of men are also available. In summer 1988, 'boil-in-the-bag' meals were introduced for soldiers in the field. Clearly such variety of foodstuffs, some of which has to be reconstituted by adding water (purifying tablets come in the pack), is a long way from the weighing out of a biscuit and cheese ration to Cromwellian soldiers.

Traditionally, soldiers have supplemented their rations with purchases from the sutlers or, when barracks were built, from traders who were

Demonstration of a barrack cooking apparatus devised by Alexis Soyer (1809–58). Soyer, who came to Britain as a refugee in 1831, was an imaginative and innovative caterer. During the Crimean War he went at his own expense to the war zone, in order to advise Florence Nightingale regarding hospital dietaries. For a time he supervised the preparation of food for the 4th Division. He was a pioneer of army cookery and set up a model kitchen in the Wellington Barracks. The cooking wagon which he invented was the forerunner of the widely used mobile field kitchen.

65

Heavy drinking was endemic amongst serving soldiers and was the cause of much army 'crime': unpunctuality, dirty kit, absence from parade, insolence to a superior, fighting and the like. Regimental canteens like this one in the later nineteenth century, run by a private contractor, did something to contain drinking within barracks, and to prevent disorderly and drunken soldiers from coming into conflict with townspeople and the civilian police.

allowed to set up canteens. Until some years after the end of the Crimean War in 1856 the army depended for all 'extras' on these private adventurers. The two official meals of the day, with the consequent long period between midday and breakfast the following morning, often meant that a great deal of drinking went on – with more business for the stall-holders who followed the army around. There was a great deal of money to be made out of satisfying the army's needs, and many sutlers and canteen owners grew rich. When these traders moved into established barracks they were charged a rent, so that in the 1840s the government was making a profit of some £65,000 a year out of its failure to take the welfare of its men seriously. Quartermasters, too, were known to line their pockets at the expense of the men to whom they issued provisions – even if the quality of the food left much to be desired, with bad meat and bread, or biscuit alive with weevils.

It was the Crimean campaign in which soldiers really went hungry, and the hardships in that war stirred the public conscience and led to the apotheosis of Florence Nightingale. Efforts were made, in several respects, to improve the lot of the common soldier. In 1863 the running of canteens was made the responsibility of individual regiments. An officer was appointed canteen president, and the day-to-day running was left to a steward chosen from amongst the sergeants. In practice many of the stewards succumbed to the temptation of making easy money. Army pay, even for a senior non-commissioned officer, was not high, and a steward was an easy target for the bribery of suppliers. Furthermore, it was not difficult to misappropriate some of the cash taken over the counter. So the canteen situation remained unsatisfactory until in 1892 Captain Lionel Fortescue, canteen president of the 17th Lancers, instituted a 'locked till' system, insisting that all purchases had to be made with the exact amount required. The till would be unlocked and checked by an officer each morning. Discrepancies were suspected when the system came into use, and Sergeant John Gardner, scrupulously honest, was appointed steward. The result was that Fortescue's system was followed by many units throughout the army.

Two years later, in 1894, Major Harry Crawfurd of the Grenadier Guards and Surgeon-Captain H.M. Ramsay, medical officer of the Scots Guards, joined Fortescue in founding the Canteen and Mess Co-operative Society with a capital of £400. Interest on this initial sum was limited to five per cent, with the remaining profits accruing to the canteen. The idea was that the Society would eventually become the recognised buying agency for the whole of the army. Despite a degree of scepticism and some ridicule from officers, the annual turnover had risen by 1900 from £4,700 to £265,000 and the Society had made considerable headway against competitors who had won much of their business through bribery. The years 1913 and 1914 saw the 'Canteen Scandal'. A sordid and half-forgotten episode in army history, it concerned allegations of bribery against employees of firms approved by the War Office, and the acceptance of bribes by some of its military customers. The allegations were proved, and a number of officers and non-commissioned officers were dismissed the service. The whole matter featured prominently in the press of the day, and the business of the Canteen and Mess Co-operative Society made rapid advances as more and more regimental canteens became members.

When war was declared in August 1914, no provision had been made for canteen organisation in the Expeditionary Force. Inevitably local traders took advantage of the situation and prices rose rapidly, particularly in areas where large numbers of men were concentrated. The War Office approached the Canteen and Mess Co-operative Society and the most reputable contractor, Richard Dickeson & Co., with a view to providing canteens in all theatres of war; and in 1915 Expeditionary Force Canteens, with the Society appointing staff and conducting the business, came into being. The venture was very successful, but the continuing expansion of the army brought more problems with contractors who were mainly concerned with making high profits as quickly as they could, and an Army Canteen Committee, with limited authority to inspect canteens, was set up. Private Edge of the 2nd Battalion, Royal Welch Fusiliers, whom we have already met, was a member of his regimental canteen staff at this period. Attempts to exercise some control over contractors and the prices they charged were largely unsuccessful, so in January 1917 the Army Canteen Committee, embracing the principles and organisation of the Society, took over as the central authority for running army canteens.

Within four months it was responsible for about two thousand canteens at home, and was actively taking over those in Gibraltar, Malta and Egypt. In the same year naval canteens came into the army organisation, and it was renamed the Navy and Army Canteen Board (NACB). Sergeant John Gardner, who had been a steward under Captain Fortescue's system, became a member of this Board. When the Royal Air Force was constituted as a separate service in 1918 its canteens, too, came under the control of the NACB. After the war, in 1920, the government decreed that canteens for the three services should be administered by a joint organisation run on co-operative lines. It was to be called Navy, Army and Air Force Institutes, and thus on 1 January 1921 NAAFI became responsible for service canteens.

During the years of uneasy peace in the 1920s and 1930s NAAFI canteens accompanied the army to stations as various as Ireland, Egypt, the Sudan, Germany, Iraq, China, Palestine, the Saar; and when war broke out in September 1939 it expanded to meet the new situation. At the outset it was a small distributive organisation with a trade of about £10 million and a staff of some 5,000: when the war ended it had grown into a major enterprise with a trade of £200 million, a staff of 120,000 serving five million customers in 10,000 establishments scattered through forty countries. Uniformed staff served in almost every theatre of war. Some became casualties and others were taken prisoner. After the war the organisation became much smaller, but the range of facilities offered to serving men and women, to say nothing of families, became wider, and included the provision of credit for the purchase of items including motor cars. Equally important was the conversion of the regimental canteen to a social club; there had been anticipations of such a change before the 1939 war, when a Corporals' Club, recreation room and writing room started to be features of the larger and more recent NAAFI premises. It would be difficult indeed to overestimate the difference that NAAFI has made to the lives of service men and women in the ranks. The regimental institute – to give it its correct title – transformed the way they lived, and there can be few who have served in the army, during peace or war, who do not look back upon NAAFI with a sense of affection and gratitude for a service that so many of us took for granted, and might even have grumbled about at the time.

Mention of army canteens would not be complete without reference to those run in both world wars by such bodies as the Church Army, the Salvation Army, YMCA and Toc H. They too offered refreshments, writing facilities, and even in some cases advice if it was sought, in locations at home and abroad. There were smaller organisations which ran mobile canteens, often serving hot drinks in small outlying units. One such body, a temperance organisation, is remembered in the words of an anonymous lance-corporal in the Ordnance Depot in Derby, who greeted their arrival each morning at about eleven with the cry 'The Rechabites are 'ere!' It was the signal to seize one's mug and queue up for tea and a piece of cake ('char and a wad') costing two or three old pence. The crew of the canteen consisted of elderly civilian volunteers.

A rush for the wet canteen, turn of the century.

A NAAFI canteen at Caen, July 1944.

One of the attractions for some who joined the army was the prospect of promotion – which meant, in most cases, better pay, an improved style of living, and always added responsibilities. A fundamental requirement for any soldier's promotion, apart from the obvious military qualities he would have to display, was an ability to read and write. In the seventeenth-century armies this was probably not so necessary, though there does seem to have been a degree of literacy amongst the troopers and private men of Cromwell's army at least. *The Souldier's Catechisme: for the Parliaments Army* was widely distributed in 1644, presumably following the success of *The Souldiers Pocket Bible* which had been similarly disseminated in the previous year. Someone was making the assumption that rank and file soldiery were able to read, at least in sufficient numbers to make such distribution worthwhile. The Cromwellian army of 'Saints', however, was exceptional, and in the following century the need for non-commissioned officers who could both read and write was increasingly felt. General Wolfe, when commanding troops in Scotland after the Jacobite rising, assumed that men promoted to the rank of corporal or sergeant would be literate, and decreed that ' . . . the orderly corporal of each company is to make a report in writing every morning.' Another order directed that ' . . . the sergeants and corporals are to give in an account in writing to the commanding officers of the companies of the manner in which the different squads mess.'

There is said to have been a regimental school at the Tower of London, but no details of it have survived. Such an institution was not, at any rate, unknown at this period. As Captain Bennett Cuthbertson, Adjutant of the 5th Foot, put it in 1768:

> From the common people (the English in particular) employing their children very early, in works of labour, their education becomes

British army post office at Constantinople, 1856. The novelist Anthony Trollope was one of many officials who were improving postal services at this period. The army overseas benefited greatly from their reforms.

totally neglected, and as the Soldiery is generally from that class, many of them (though otherwise properly qualified for non-commission-officers) can neither read nor write, which being absolutely necessary for those employed as such, it would be of infinite improvement, if (as is the case, in the Corps of Scotch Hollanders) every Regiment was to establish a school, under the management of some old Soldier qualified for such an undertaking, and to be supported by voluntary contributions from the Officers; by which means, not only the Soldiers, who were desirous of improvement, might be taught to read and write, but also the children of the Regiment; which institution, besides the advantage it must always be, to have a number of men so far well qualified for non-commission-officers, would likewise be a real charity, by educating children, who from the poverty of their parents, must ever remain in a state of ignorance.

The link between education and promotion was made even more apparent in the standing orders of the 25th Foot in 1804:

> The non-commissioned officers that may not be perfectly proficient in their writing, keeping accounts, spelling, etc., are expected to attend (i.e. school). Boys are ordered to go to school until they are dismissed by the Adjutant; and it is strongly recommended to the Private Soldiers to take the earliest opportunity of going to school, as . . . those who make the greatest proficiency there will be the first for promotion.

The wording here is interesting. Boys are ordered; private soldiers are encouraged; non-commissioned officers are expected to study. There were sound reasons for educating soldiers. While an older generation of officers typified by Captain Plume in *The Recruiting Officer* might have said 'A fellow that can write can draw petitions', the fact was that the satisfactory running of a regiment demanded NCOs who could read orders, copy them out, and on occasion cast simple accounts. With soldiers on detachment throughout the country, often in small parties under a sergeant or a corporal, quartered at inns whose landlords were required by law to furnish straw, candles, food and drink, opportunities for cheating were many. An illiterate NCO was helpless: one who was literate could check that the right amounts were supplied and be precise about the payments involved. The more men who achieved a basic literacy, the greater was the pool of possible candidates for promotion.

There was yet another reason, at the end of the eighteenth century, for regarding an 'educated soldier' as an ideal to be striven for. Enlightened and far-seeing infantry officers who had fought in the forests of America began to realise that close order drill, which trained men to stand unthinkingly in line under fire and often to be killed as a result, was not the most satisfactory way to train men to face a resourceful foe who made effective use of ground and other sorts of cover. Troops would have to be taught to take initiatives in action, and this implied a delicate balance between the established methods of infantry training and possible new ones with some stress on individuality. The army went some way towards striking such a balance by raising, in August 1800, an Experimental Corps of Riflemen from selected detachments of other regiments. This became the 95th Foot in 1803, and later the Rifle Brigade. Instead of advancing across open ground in straight lines, dressed as they went by sergeants and firing their muskets in volleys, the riflemen learned, among other skills, to advance in extended order and to act, when necessary, as sharpshooters.

This is the period when we begin to become aware of highly articulate and able men serving in the ranks of the army. Best known is probably William Cobbett, who tells us that he was 'raised from corporal to sergeant-major, over the heads of thirty sergeants'. He had taught himself the rudiments of English grammar while he was a recruit. Amongst others who wrote memoirs or letters which have survived are Sergeant Roger Lamb, Sergeant William Wheeler, Sergeant John Cooper; and there was Sergeant Thomas Borrow, whose son George wrote an account of his father in *Lavengro*. Cobbett described another:

> There was one of our sergeants whose name was Smaller, and who was a Yorkshire man, who began learning his ABC (under my direction), and who, at the end of the year, was as correct a writer as I ever saw in my life. He was about my own age; he was promoted as soon as he could write and read; and he well deserved it, for he was more fit to command a regiment than any Colonel or Major that I ever saw.

Such men as these were serving soldiers, and had been promoted long before the army came to terms with the problem of educating its men at a level beyond that of a regimental school supervised by the chaplain. The pattern of educating men for promotion to higher rank was irrevocably

A sergeant of the Royal Irish Fusiliers writing home, Egypt, 1882. The writer has wrapped a piece of gauze around his head to protect it from flies.

71

set by the early years of the nineteenth century.

In 1809 the commanding officer of the Bedford Militia decided to make compulsory the attendance of his non-commissioned officers at school. He insisted, moreover, that they should pay a few pence a week for tuition. This was an irregular order, and some of the militiamen demurred. Corporal Tompkins did not attend because he thought that Sergeant-Major Warner, who was to provide the instruction, was only 'a pretty midlingish scholar'. An elderly corporal, Dickens Prigmore, who had 'been a soldier going on twenty-one years', said that while his fingers were too stiff for a pen 'they are lissom enough for a firelock', and he did not like the way children laughed at him on his way to school. Sergeant Richard Warden was up in arms too, and vociferously encouraged a fellow sergeant, John Cooper, to join him in his protest: 'Damn your eyes Jack . . . don't go to school, for I'll be damned if I do. I will soldier with anybody, but I won't be made a boy of.' As a result of his violent language Warden was taken under escort to the town gaol and faced a court martial – which sensibly took the view that the whole thing was a storm in a teacup and acquitted him. Warden then opened legal proceedings for false imprisonment, was awarded damages, and went off to enlist in the 3rd King's Own Dragoons. The case, known as Warden v. Bailey, had a profound effect on the development of education in the army, for the judge gave a ruling which was to bedevil it for some years to come: 'It is no part of the military duty to attend a school, and learn to read and write. If writing is necessary to corporals and sergeants, the superior officers must select men who can read and write.' The last appeal in Warden v. Bailey was heard in 1811, and a few months later a letter went out from the Adjutant-General to all commanding officers, directing them to establish a regimental school in each battalion or corps 'for the instruction of young soldiers, and the children of soldiers'. Legal opinion had made it impossible for the army to do more. Basic educational facilities would be provided for the men who chose to make use of them and who were keen to rise in the army.

When the Duke of Wellington, in 1849, ordered that all army recruits must attend school daily during their period of initial training, Law Officers of the Crown, while admitting the necessity for compulsory education in the army, regarded the order as illegal. (Eventually the law was changed, and from 1879 it was a statutory offence for a soldier not to attend school if he had been ordered to do so.) The Duke of Wellington also directed that no soldier who had not completed his school course should be promoted – unless in the field – to the rank of corporal.

By the 1860s a new 4th Class Certificate was instituted to mark the stage at which the recruit was exempt from any further compulsory education. At the same time 3rd and 2nd Class Certificates were listed among the qualifications required for promotion to corporal and sergeant. Army reforms in the 1870s brought various changes, including the abolition of the 4th Class Certificate, and from 1890 onwards a private soldier could not draw his full rate of proficiency pay until he had gained a 3rd Class Certificate. Further developments came, particularly between

1920 and 1939, when 3rd, 2nd, 1st and 'Special' Certificates covering the spectrum of education from bare literacy to university entrance strengthened the palpable link between education and promotion. It is a connection that has more validity than ever in the army of the 1980s.

Not very much is known about the men who were promoted in the armies of seventeenth-century England, nor about the badges of rank that they wore. Sergeant Nehemiah Wharton has already been mentioned. Between August and October 1642 he wrote a series of letters to Mr George Willingham, a merchant at the Golden Anchor in St Swithin's Lane, London, describing his experience while serving with the Parliamentary army. Wharton may formerly have been an apprentice or a servant – there is little to go on in his letters, but his voice is that of the common soldier, one of the very few that have come down to us from the Great Rebellion. We have glimpsed an anonymous sergeant engaged on weighing out the ration of cheese and biscuit in an upstairs room, and names occasionally turn up in court martial records, but we know very little of the non-commissioned officers and men at this period. According to Thomas Gumble, whose biography *The Life of George Monck, Duke of Albermarle* was published in 1671, great care was taken in Monck's regiment (first raised in 1650) with the selection of sergeants and corporals 'who are the eyes and hands of every company'. In addition to their military duties these non-commissioned officers had the task of explaining to the rank and file why Monck was opposing Lambert's army in England. Those who carried this out efficiently were promised promotion – 'a motive that never fails', added Gumble.

A less agreeable light is cast on the non-commissioned officer's life by the case of Abraham Randall, a soldier in Captain Parker's company in Monck's regiment. His sergeant (whose name we do not know) testified that when the company was drawn up in church at Dundee, Randall

> being playing and abusing his fellow soliders, this deponent told him if hee continued in it hee would strike him. To which Randall said, "Doe as you dare, I will strike you againe." Whereupon this deponent struck him a box in the eare, upon which Randall struck him againe several times, till he was parted by Corporal Bond, but afterwards this deponent being lighting a pipe of tobacco Randall fell upon him again.

Another soldier, John Browne, then intervened saying that if he had been Randall he would have broken his stick over the sergeant's head. Discipline was strict in Monck's regiment, and both insubordinate soldiers were punished.

About half way through the eighteenth century we begin to gain a clearer view of the men who became non-commissioned officers, because a few of them kept diaries or, when they had left the service, wrote their memoirs. The earliest diarist was Corporal William Todd, who served with the 30th Foot from 1749 to 1758, and with the 12th Foot in 1761. The extant portions of his diary, transcribed by his daughter Peggie, cover several years of peace-time soldiering, mostly in Ireland; the expeditions in 1757 and 1758 to Rochefort and St Malo and Cherbourg; then, finally, service in Westphalia during 1761. Despite the fact that when he died in 1763 aged thirty-eight Todd was described in the parish register as a 'Labourer', he seems to have been a man of some education. In 1754 he acted as a regimental schoolmaster, having joined the regular army after service in the militia during the Jacobite rising of 1745.

When his regiment was under canvas at Chatham in 1756, Todd was already a corporal, and one of his duties was to instruct the men in camp procedure. Five private soldiers shared a tent, while each corporal and each sergeant had one of his own. To maintain discipline the commanding officer ordered that sergeants were not to drink with corporals, nor corporals with the men. This order may have led Todd to propose the establishment of a Corporals' Club which met every Thursday after roll call – an example which was soon followed by the sergeants of the regiment. It was at about this time that Todd was appointed Drill Corporal and had 'no other duty but exercising recruits'. In 1758 he was granted leave, and the journey from Canterbury, where he was then stationed, to his Yorkshire home took him nearly a fortnight. The first part of Todd's diary ends abruptly at the close of the same year.

The other surviving portion, covering 1761, starts with Todd serving as a private soldier with the 12th Foot. Just why he had been transferred to another regiment and reduced to the ranks he does not tell us. Perhaps the battalion to which he was drafted had suffered heavy casualties, and the loss of rank may well have been the result of drinking. As he tells us, his officer had warned him to take 'more care of getting too much liquor', and told him that as he was 'near of getting preferr'd' he would do well to 'refrain himself from being any ways intoxicated'. In May he was restored to the rank of corporal. His company commander had received a good report of him from his previous regiment, the 30th, and he was well able to read and write. Indeed, since some of his fellow NCOs could 'scarce write that anyone can read', this accomplishment seems to have been a factor in his promotion. The event was celebrated by his fellow corporals who became 'very merry' drinking punch. At this period, too, new 'cloathing' was issued to the battalion, and especial care was taken to see that the uniforms of all NCOs were properly fitted.

In June the corporal of the regimental pioneers died, and this left a vacancy for which there was little competition. The pioneers' duty was hard and dangerous, particularly when they were 'out in front to cut down wood, make facines and bridges and roads through woods', and the pioneers were also under the orders of the Quartermaster, Lieutenant Barlow, notorious throughout the 12th for his severity. Todd, who had served as a pioneer, was selected for the vacancy, and was not too pleased 'as knowing we was very often in danger of being surprized by the enemy.' He was with the pioneers during the Battle of Vellinghausen, fought on 15 and 16 July, and he describes how, when food was running short, further supplies were found in the haversacks of dead French soldiers. Some time after the engagement Todd fell foul of Lieutenant Barlow. One of the pioneers' tasks was to screen the officers' latrines with boughs to ensure privacy, and the Quartermaster, dissatisfied with the way the work had been done, put Todd, as the NCO in charge, under arrest. When brought before his company commander Todd pointed out that his men had also to erect the officers' mess tent and see to their kitchen; and finally he asked to be relieved of his duties as pioneer corporal. The major commanding the company smoothed things over, and Todd went back to duty, emerging from the affair with assurances that he was a proficient pioneer corporal. His relationship with Barlow subsequently improved, though Todd regarded him as 'a very tedious gentleman'.

One of the perquisites of the job was that pioneers were allowed to charge for the wood they provided for the officers' kitchen. Another was that pioneers detailed for woodcutting were able sometimes to augment their ration of beef and bacon with a selection of poultry. Todd has something to say about the hardships of campaigning – a camp he had helped to construct became a sea of mud, and sometimes the bread ration was mouldy – but his diary adds little to our knowledge of the campaigns in which he was involved. It does, however, tell us about the daily life of an army corporal over a period of eleven or twelve years in the eighteenth century. Two questions arise from the diary: what did the army officially require of its corporals, and what badges did they wear to show their rank?

General Wolfe's orders issued in the mid-eighteenth century placed a great deal of stress on the role of the corporal in running an efficient unit: 'The corporals to be very careful to warn the men for exercise and all other duties; and the first man that absents himself, either from exercise or a review, shall immediately be tried . . . ' And again:

The 25th Foot on parade in Minorca in about 1771. On the extreme right is the commanding officer speaking to the sergeant-major, hat in hand, who stands to his left. The drum major is also visible. To the left, the men with knots on their shoulders are corporals. Their headgear is different from that of the privates.

Infantry lance-corporals, *c.* 1938. Obtaining one stripe, paid or unpaid, represented the first step on the ladder of promotion. Subject to suitability and a vacancy, a lance-corporal could be promoted to the rank of corporal with two stripes. In the Royal Artillery the equivalents are lance-bombardier and bombardier.

The orderly corporal of each company is to make a report in writing every morning before the guard mounts, to his captain or command-ing officer, of the men's names that are to mount guard, the men sick in hospital or in their quarters, and of anything else that is proper to be reported; this is to be the constant practice of the regiment.

The most fundamental duty of corporals was to see that orders were obeyed with what Wolfe called 'alacrity and diligence'. It is one, often with added responsibilities, that they perform in the army today.

As his badge of rank Todd would have worn either a worsted shoulder knot ('promoted to the knot' was an eighteenth-century expression for promotion to corporal), or an epaulette. There were differences in pattern and colour between regiments, and there seems to have been no unifor-mity in non-commissioned officers' badges of rank throughout the army. Commanding officers, apparently, exercised considerable discretion, though not total control, in this respect. Sergeants were distinguished by more elaborately decorated coats. In 1813 Corporal Wheeler, serving in the Peninsula in Wellington's army, was promoted sergeant some time after such promotion was due, largely because of his own diffidence and doubts. His adjutant told him impatiently that he was 'a damn'd fool' and might have had a sergeant's coat much sooner. Hats and sashes were also used to designate a sergeant's rank, and it was not until after the Battle of Waterloo in 1815 that chevrons, or 'stripes' in army parlance, were used throughout the army to show the rank of a non-commissioned officer. The earliest record of the use of chevrons that I have been able to trace was in the 43rd Foot, where they were being worn in the shape of a letter 'V' reversed in 1795.

Serving soldiers have always been conscious of rank, and distinctions are comprehended immediately. This was even true in the nineteenth-century army, where there was a proliferation of non-commissioned ranks and appointments, and it continues in the modern army. While civilians might find it difficult to distinguish between an RQMS and an SQMS (Regimental Quartermaster Sergeant and Staff Quartermaster Sergeant), or between an RSM and a Sub-Conductor (Regiment Sergeant Major and 1st Class Warrant Officer, Royal Army Ordnance Corps), soldiers can almost always do so, and can recognise at once the badges of rank that may be worn on the upper or lower sleeve.

However complex the pattern of ranks and badges might become, the first step in promotion was the most important and would, for a majority of soldiers, mean becoming a lance-corporal. The term 'lance' requires some explanation. Sir James Turner in his *Pallas Armata* (1653) describes it in these words:

The lance corporal was originally a man at arms or trooper, who having broken his lance on the enemy, and lost his horse in fight, was entertained, as a volunteer assistant to a captain of foot, receiving his pay as a trooper, until he could remount himself; from being the companion of the captain, he was soon degraded to the assistant of the corporal, and at present does the duty of that officer, on the pay of a private soldier.

When Corporal Todd joined the pioneers, his place in the rifle company was taken by a 'Lance' who would, if satisfactory in carrying out his duties, be next in line for promotion to full corporal. Because it represented the first step on the ladder there was never a shortage of men ready to accept such an appointment; and when, in the 1870s, extra pay for lance-corporals was introduced, the prospect became even more attractive.

Changes in the way of life of a private who took this step are well described by John Acland. He became a lance-corporal in the 1870s, and spoke with pride of his 'one stripe', the outward sign of his authority, worn on the sleeve of his tunic above the elbow:

> The one great change in my work now was that I could never be asked to do any real 'fatigue work' . . . At coal-carrying and other fatigues I had only to take part by superintending, and seeing that the men did the work properly . . . Although I have just said that lance-corporals did not have to use their hands very much, there is no doubt that they have to use their feet . . . If anything extra had to be done, a lance-corporal would certainly have to do it, whether it were taking messages for officers on duty – marching small parties of men, looking after prisoners etc.

Another soldier, John Shipp, recalled his own promotion from private to full corporal at a somewhat earlier date, and the same sense of pride in achievement runs through his account (*The Path of Glory*, 1843; 1969):

> A corporal has to take command of small guards: is privileged to visit the sentinels whenever he pleases; his suggestions are frequently attended to by his superiors; and his orders must be promptly obeyed by those below him. There is certainly a pleasure in all this, and a man rises proportionately in his own esteem. In short, to confess the truth I now looked upon a drum-boy as little better than his drum.

Finally, there was a corporal in the army in the mid-1980s who described

Barrack room in Catterick Camp, 1955. The corporal in charge is seated to the left of the fireplace; to its right is standing his assistant, a lance-corporal.

Ante-room of a sergeants' mess in India early in this century. Such institutions in the sub-continent were usually very much more comfortable than in barracks at home. They were more spacious and would employ considerable numbers of Indians as cooks, waiters, barmen and cleaners.

being a corporal as 'the best rank you can have'. With such enthusiasm, he will almost certainly be promoted to sergeant.

Becoming a sergeant was an important promotion, whether it was from corporal to the appointment of lance sergeant, or advancement to the full rank. 'The sergeant', said Robert Blatchford, who served as one in the 103rd Foot, 'is a soldier and the private is a soldier; but there is a difference between them beyond the difference of pay, position, responsibility and dress. The sergeant might belong to a different race' (*My Life in the Army*, n.d.; 1910). There is a degree of hyperbole here, but the statement, made in late Victorian times, remains largely true. Equally, Blatchford's contention that 'sergeants are the most responsible men in the army' carries with it, despite some overstatement, a great deal of truth. Without sergeants, quartermaster sergeants, sergeants-major, other senior NCOs and warrant officers, the organisation of the army would soon disintegrate. Nobody put it better than John Williamson, an eighteenth-century writer on military affairs, who described them as the 'nerves and sinews of the corps'.

The newly promoted sergeant, traditionally, moves into new quarters which he may share with two or three others, or he may perhaps have a room to himself. No longer does he have the need to make up his bed each morning, with blankets folded and kit laid out for inspection. The sergeant may leave his bed as he wishes, and his quarters may be inspected only if prior notice is given. Going in and out of barracks is normally unrestricted, and there are other privileges; but the most important privilege of all is membership of the sergeants' mess. The significance of this in the life of any army unit is twofold. First there is the enhancement of the sergeant's status and that of other senior ranks by setting them visibly apart, and thus underlining the hierarchical structure of rank and discipline without which the army could not function, while at the same time the mess remains for its members a club of equals. Secondly, it provides a place where senior non-commissioned officers and warrant officers may meet their commissioned counterparts over a drink and talk of professional matters of mutual interest. Such contact can take place only if the officer is invited into the sergeants' mess, and the reverse process of sergeants being invited into the officers' mess is not permitted. The sergeants' mess, then, provides a comfortable milieu for members to take their meals together, together with recreational facilities and, sometimes, sleeping quarters. As an institution it has a fairly short history, belonging largely to the great period of barrack building which followed the end of the Crimean War. Its origins are not altogether clear. The commanding officer of the 30th Regiment in 1756 as we have seen earlier, without quite realising that he was doing so, may have taken one of the first steps towards its establishment. We are on firmer ground when we look at the period after the Battle of Waterloo in 1815. In the following year at Windsor there was a three-day celebration to mark the first anniversary of the battle, when the Royal Horse Guards and a battalion of the Grenadier Guards were in garrison. The officers of the latter unit gave an entertainment to a distinguished group of guests which included the Duke of York. A contemporary observer remarked that 'Elegance and taste predominated in the decoration. The room fitted up was a large one, usually occupied by the Sergeants.' Since no provision was officially made for sergeants' messes at this time, it seems clear that in Windsor these senior NCOs were looking after themselves very well.

We find another indication that they did so in the testimony of an old man, Mr John Tully, who had been a civilian Forage Master to the 1st Life Guards in the reign of Queen Victoria. His memories went back a long way, and he recalled that at Regent's Park Barracks, London, before there was a sergeants' mess, there was a wicket gate direct from the barracks into the 'Crown and Anchor' public house next door, where a private room was reserved for the sergeants.

The earliest mention of such a mess in barracks that I have found is in the Standing Orders of the 87th or Prince of Wales Own Irish Fusiliers, published in 1827. Under 'Messing' appeared the following paragraph:

> It is the wish of the lieutenant colonel to see the sergeants mess conducted with the greatest practical comfort and respectability; it will be regulated by a code of rules sanctioned by the lieutenant colonel, and hung up in the mess room; the sergeants will breakfast and dine half an hour later than the men.

Standing Orders for the regiment published five years earlier, in 1822, had made no mention of a sergeants' mess.

> After six years of barrack life the change was a very marked one; the food was much superior, and there were mess waiters to attend to our requirements. I acquired a share in a room with two other sergeants; never again did I groom a horse for I had a batman now to look after me and furbish up my traps, and there were the club-like conveniences of the mess to make the evenings pass pleasantly.

Both men, it will be seen, stressed the difference in their lives after they became sergeants. Acland, who became an officer, took the new life as no more than his due, while the tone of Mole's writing is rather different. The pleasure he takes in becoming a sergeant is almost palpable – he went on to become a troop sergeant-major. His reference to pleasant evenings in the mess is one of the few we have about the social life of these institutions. A not very distinguished poem by James Thomson ('B.V.'), who served as a non-commissioned army schoolmaster in the late nineteenth century, recalls a night in the mess:

> With the old black pipe and the steaming glass,
> And a toast to the health of each sonsie lass,
> And a right jolly set the toast to pass,
>   Drink, boys, drink!

Field Marshal Sir William Robertson looked back on his service with the 16th (Queen's) Lancers in York in about 1880 when, as he wrote: 'I was promoted lance-sergeant (or provisional sergeant), thus becoming a member of the sergeants' mess and terminating my life with the men.' He said – characteristically, perhaps – very little about how his life changed, except to mention that he had a batman who was paid six shillings (30p) a month by the government to look after his horse, accoutrements and equipment. Robertson saw his advancement rather single-mindedly, as a means of extending his professional competence as a soldier. As a sergeant he was sent to a signal school, and having passed out top of his course he was made assistant instructor of the regimental signallers – whose standard, he tells us, was very low. In 1885 Robertson became troop sergeant-major, and in his autobiography, *From Private to Field Marshal* (1921), wrote about the duties which went with this rank:

> A troop sergeant-major occupies a position which enables him to exert, for good or evil, great influence over his men. It is said that the non-commissioned officer is the backbone of the army, but it is equally true that he can do much harm unless he is strictly impartial and identifies himself with the interests of his men.

From the rank of sergeant a non-commissioned officer might, if he was good at his job and fortunate to be found when a vacancy occurred, be promoted sergeant-major, quartermaster sergeant or pay sergeant. Corporal William Todd, whose diary has already been referred to, spoke in 1756 of 'the Sergeant Major of our company', but it is difficult to know precisely what he meant by this because just over a century later the Standing Orders of the 4th 'The King's Own' Regiment refer only to one sergeant-major and one quartermaster sergeant for the entire battalion. The sergeant-major assisted the adjutant, while the quartermaster sergeant assisted the officer who acted as quartermaster to the unit. It was not until the last decades of the nineteenth century that warrant officers – who messed with the sergeants – were introduced into the army, and at this point the hierarchy of non-commissioned rank becomes complex, no less than the badges which distinguish them. What this meant in practical terms for men in the ranks was that the ladder of promotion was much enhanced, and offered a wide range of opportunity. Within infantry and cavalry units company and troop sergeants-major were introduced; and in the more technical arms – supply, engineers or artillery – the number of technical posts for skilled tradesmen, who might be sergeants, staff sergeants or warrant officers, increased considerably. Following the Cardwell reforms of the 1870s the army was beginning to offer a real career to recruits, and by about 1900 the outlook for an able and literate man who wished to make a career in the service had improved out of all recognition.

In some respects, though, the army does not change greatly. For the infantry private soldier, guardsman or rifleman, time will be spent cleaning kit and weapons, mounting guard, doing sentry go or gate duty, and also just hanging about. The more technical corps may offer something different, but in most cases the basic elements of repetition, routine and 'spit and polish' are still part of the soldier's daily round. The problems posed by boredom amongst rank and file soldiers have never been satisfactorily solved, and it is hard to see how they can be. While undergoing training there is much to do and much to be learned, with a great deal of it novel and interesting; but for trained men things are different. How many men serving in Germany think it worthwhile to learn the language? How many young soldiers are temperamentally or educationally equipped to come to terms with what is often the long tedium of garrison life in peacetime? There are no clear answers to either of these questions, nor is it certain how the army of today should tackle them.

A night out in Colchester, 1956. Three privates decide whether they can afford to go to the cinema.

Chapter 4

'LADIES, WIVES AND WOMEN'

'Officers and their ladies; sergeants and their wives; soldiers and their women . . . ' This phrase, long outmoded, reflects a scale of values implicit in some army attitudes during much of the nineteenth century and in the earlier years of the twentieth. So far as the preceding centuries are concerned we know little. There were camp followers and married officers – we can be certain of this because the Duke of Marlborough concerned himself with the care of officers' widows, and towards the end of Queen Anne's reign the state did begin to accept some responsibility for them; but for other army dependants there was the workhouse as a last resort. The women, and for that matter the children, remain largely unknown to us.

Armies in garrison or on the march have always attracted hangers-on, and a majority of these have been women. There would be soldiers' wives who, when their husbands enlisted, had little choice but to follow them. Life was hard, and they were barely recognised by the army; but the care of children, cooking, uniform repair and laundry work could, if carried out for officers, be the source of a precariously small extra income. Women sometimes accompanied their men because, in theory at least, the army was not a bad proposition for poor families. For the soldier there was the promise of pay – however miserly – food and even a new doublet, although the reality, with constant arrears of pay and inadequate provisions, often fell short of the ideal. There was, moreover, only the remotest chance of a pension if the man should be killed in action. For wives and children the baggage trains of seventeenth-century armies could be havens (and not for them alone – camp followers of all kinds, whores, petty criminals, tradespeople intent upon selling food and drink to the soldiers and plying other trades, all went along). The roads, particularly for women travelling alone, could be fraught with danger, and there was a degree of safety to be found in the noise, bustle and anonymity of the baggage train. Besides, women who stayed at home when their husbands had 'gone for a soldier' could end up like Elizabeth Newton of Leicester, with six small children and 'in extreme want'. Her only recourse was to apply for relief from the parish officers of St Margaret's Church. Another woman, Margery Roberts, became a pick-pocket when her husband enlisted. On the other hand, some women were otherwise resourceful: the wives of Sergeant Fletcher and Sergeant Hirst, for example, turned to ale-house keeping.

When the Parliamentary army entered Stafford in December 1643 the number of soldiers' dependants accompanying it caused the local authorities some alarm, and they ordered 'that from henceforth no soldier whatsoever shall bring in his wife and family to inhabit here unless they do first give sufficient security that they shall not be chargeable to the said Towne and provide sufficient provision for a quarter of a years before hand . . . '

In 1647 an army of some 20,000 passed through St Albans on its way from Royston to London. Despite the Parliamentary sympathies of most people in the town, the number of men and camp followers caused considerable apprehension among the residents, particularly as many of

OPPOSITE:
Annual ball of senior non-commissioned officers (sergeants, staff sergeants, sergeants-major) at the Royal Artillery School, Woolwich, 1859. Such festivities were conducted with considerable formality, and it was customary for the commandant to put in a brief appearance as guest of honour. On this occasion, the dancing went on 'with great spirit' until six o'clock the next morning.

the dependants stayed on when the army had gone on its way. Any sudden influx of indigent people placed an intolerable burden on a settled community and its charities. Amongst the camp followers, too, there might be itinerant women preachers whose presence in society at large in the years following the Civil War was sufficiently obvious to attract the angry attention of Thomas Edwards, a noted polemic writer of the mid-1640s.

There were even one or two women who enlisted. In 1657 the officer commanding the garrison at Ayr reported that a young woman from Lincolnshire named Anne Dymoke had served for several weeks in his regiment. 'I can perceive', he wrote, 'nothing but modesty in her carriage since she has been with us.' Several contemporary ballads featured women soldiers: 'The Famous Woman Drummer', 'The Soldier's Delight or the She-Volunteer', 'The Maiden Warrior' and 'Pretty Polly Oliver'. Another, 'The Gallant She-Soldier', tells us something about a soldier's life:

> With musket on her shoulder, her part she acted then,
> And every-one supposed that she had been a man;
> Her bandeleers about her neck, and sword hang'd by her side,
> In many brave adventures her valour have been tried.
>
> For exercising of her arms, good skill indeed had she,
> And known to be as active as any one could be,
> For firing of a musket, or beating of a drum,
> She might compare assuredly with any one that come.
>
> For other manly practices she gain'd the love of all,
> For leaping and for running or wrestling for a fall,
> For cudgels or for cuffing, if that occasion were,
> There's hardly one of ten men that might with her compare.
>
> Yet civill in her carriage and modest still was she,
> But with her fellow souldiers she oft would merry be;
> She would drink and take tobacco, and spend her money too
> When an occasion served, that she had nothing else to do.

A helping hand in camp, the Peninsula, 1803.

Towards the end of the seventeenth century the position of army wives began to be regularised. It was widely accepted that soldiers were not encouraged to marry, and recruiting parties were forbidden to take married men, but the fact remained that many men were married and in 1694 each company of the Royal Marines was permitted to take three soldiers' wives on the strength. This was probably the first step in the acceptance by military authority of marriage in the lower ranks of the army. The women in question must have been tough: in a quarrel between two of them, one 'almost killed another . . . with a grenadier's hatchet.'

The number of women carried on the strength of regiments increased during the eighteenth century. Commanding generals, though nearly always reluctantly, realised that they had a role to play – necessary, as Sir William Johnson put it in 1755, 'to wash and mend'. They did, in fact, rather more than this. Some worked as cooks and some as hospital nurses; and they might, in addition, hire themselves out as servants to officers' families, for they were free to seek any employment in camp or outside it. As always, there were large numbers of camp followers who, unlike the few army wives, were not entitled to an issue of 'the King's victuals'. Not much is known about any of these women, but some were permitted to accompany their menfolk when the regiment went on foreign service. Between 1755 (perhaps even earlier) and 1783 there were army wives in America. One of them, Martha May, wrote in a petition addressed to Colonel Henry Bouquet in June 1758: 'I have been a Wife 22 Years and have Traveld with my Husband every Place or Country the Company Marcht too.' Mrs May is one of the few soldiers' wives of this period whose name is known to us. Perhaps she was present at the siege of Quebec in 1760 when, despite official indifference, women were commanded to remain in barracks and to act as cooks and nurses. Or she may have been one of those who assisted on the ramparts when ten women per regiment were 'ordered immediately to join the artillery; they will be employed in sowing up sand-bags, and making wads from old junk for the guns.' Such women gained little appreciation for their labour. A contemporary, Benjamin Thompson, noted that the Continental troops were dirty in comparison with their British counterparts, and put this down to the fact that the Americans had 'no women in the camp to do washing for the men'. This seems to be the nearest they came in their own day to an acknowledgment that army women played a role.

A she-soldier, 1780.

The first army wives about whom we have any real knowledge are those who accompanied Wellington's army fighting the French in Portugal and Spain. The numbers involved were small: six wives, with their small children, were allowed to go with each company. When the 23rd Regiment of Foot sailed from Falmouth for Corunna there were forty-eight women and twenty children, with a total strength of forty sergeants, nineteen drummers and 575 private soldiers. This, in fact, was a high number of women. In November 1813 a return of British women with the 4th Division shows that the 7th Fusiliers had seventeen, the 20th had twenty-two, the 23rd Fusiliers twenty-five, the 27th thirty-four, the 40th twenty-four, the 48th nineteen, and a single company of the 60th had only two. Those women who accompanied their menfolk were chosen by lot. On the last evening before a regiment embarked, tickets inscribed 'To go' and 'Not to go' were put into a hat and drawn out by the individual wives. It was like a raffle with a few lucky winners, and with the unsuccessful ones facing a very uncertain future indeed. There was no administrative mechanism by which a soldier serving abroad could have a proportion of his wage paid to a wife or dependants at home. Henry Mayhew, chronicler of the London poor, was told years later, in the 1850s, by a prostitute that she had been the wife of a soldier whose regiment was ordered to India. She had not drawn a lucky ticket, and claimed that she had been reduced to her present calling in order to maintain her family. It is a story that seems inherently true, given the difficulties she would have faced in obtaining employment and the low esteem in which both 'common soldiers' and their 'women' were held by society.

The regulations which allowed women to accompany their husbands on active service were based upon utility above anything else. As we have seen, they were expected to cook, do laundry work, repair clothes, tend the wounded — notwithstanding the judgment of Captain Wall of the Royal Artillery, who wrote in his diary: 'It is a most mistaken idea to suppose that women can possibly be of the smallest use to an Army on active service. The supposition of their washing for the soldiers is a delusion . . . ' As a critic Wall did have a point, for some of the women were undisciplined. There were Mrs Skiddy, Mrs Flynn and Mrs Wheel who, during the retreat from Burgos to Portugal, persisted in blocking with their donkeys the narrow paths along which the army was moving. The provost-marshal, an officer responsible for discipline, had to intervene. There were also, inevitably perhaps, cases of drunkenness; but for the most part these women seem to have behaved with great courage, even if their loyalty to their husbands sometimes conflicted with the efficient running of the army. It goes without saying that they faced conditions of danger and considerable hardship. At least two wives were killed: the wife of Sergeant Maiby of the 51st Light Infantry was struck by a shell while she was eating breakfast, and the wife of an unnamed fusilier was killed at the Battle of Salamanca. Mrs Munday, whose husband was Orderly Room Sergeant of the 28th, carried a lapdog in a basket over her arm during the long, arduous marches, and brought it safely back to England. Another woman, who had been with the 20th for about ten years, went missing one night along the road to Corunna, leaving her daughter to trudge on alone, and was never heard of again. Then there was Mrs Reston at Cadiz in 1810, who performed several acts of bravery under fire and assisted in the treatment of badly wounded soldiers, having first left her four-year-old son in a bomb-proof shelter. Such indomitable and courageous women were remembered in the memoirs of several Peninsular veterans.

For many of them, widowhood was an ever-present hazard. The widow of Sergeant Dunn of the 68th, for example, lost five husbands altogether — there was no shortage of offers for a widow. One young woman who had attended the burial of her husband was met on her return to bivouac by a sergeant who asked her to marry him. She burst into tears at once . . . they were tears of regret, for she had already accepted the hand of a corporal in charge of the squad which had fired a volley over the grave of her dead husband.

Even harder to trace than the small number of wives who accompanied their husbands to the Peninsular War are the camp followers and prostitutes who have from earliest times played an important, if unacknowledged, role in army life. So far as the seventeenth and eighteenth centuries are concerned there is little enough to go on, but when we come to the nineteenth century there are indications that prostitution and the resulting venereal disease constituted a considerable problem. Henry Mayhew put the matter succinctly: 'The evil effects of the want of some system to regulate prostitution in England is perhaps more shown amongst the army

Washing in camp, the Peninsula, 1803. See A. Brett-James *Life in Wellington's Army*, 1972, ch.17.

then any other class.' He quoted some statistics which he had taken from *Prostitution* (1857) by William Acton. From 1837 to 1847 the aggregate strengths of Cavalry, Foot Guards and Infantry was 254,597. Over this period there were 65,683 cases of venereal disease, and seventeen of these patients died. This meant an average of 257 men per 1000 serving soldiers admitted to military hospital with a sexually transmitted disease. Behind these alarming statistics there lurked an uncomfortable reality. Not only was prostitution rife in Victorian England, but there was also an unwillingness on the part of government and Church to discuss the matter except in terms of outraged morality. This kind of hypocrisy was reflected equally in the negative attitude of the army authorities to the whole question of 'other ranks' marriage, and to their refusal to set up brothels where prostitutes could at least be inspected by Medical Officers. The attitude persisted into the Second World War, when General (as he then was) Montgomery was characterised by some sections of the popular press in the United Kingdom as the 'Love General' and attacked because he advocated a realistic approach to the sexual needs of his Desert Army. It is probable that if some other 'scandal' concerning the ineptitude of a serving general had not taken the fancy of such newspapers, Montgomery might have been relieved of his command.

For too long the army clung to the view that 'Commanding Officers should be urged to encourage in every way all forms of athletic amusement, as physical fatigue acts as a deterrent to sexual indulgence.' These were the words of the Army Sanitary Commission in India towards the end of the nineteenth century, but they must have expressed the feelings of officers commanding troops at home. They were largely irrelevant in each country. The fact was that welfare services were rudimentary, and soldiers were poorly paid. As Henry Mayhew put it some decades earlier:

ABOVE:
Loading a baggage cart prior to a move, 1802. The operation is being supervised by a sergeant (on the extreme right), identifiable by the halberd he is holding.

BELOW:
On the move.

The women who are patronized by soldiers are, as a matter of course, very badly paid; for how can a soldier out of his very scanty allowance, generally little exceeding a shilling a day, afford to supply a woman with means adequate for her existence? It follows from this state of things, that a woman may, or more correctly must, be intimate with several men in one evening . . .

One way in which venereal infection might be avoided was by association with women who were not prostitutes. Mayhew described such women as 'amateurs' – nursemaids, shop-girls, milliners, servants, who could be picked up at 'dancing academies' and to whom the general title 'Dolly-mops' was given. Nursemaids, apparently, were the object of many soliders' attentions, for they had to walk their charges in the park and could thus easily be accosted. An intimate relationship between a soldier and a servant girl was not, of course, necessarily based upon money, and this fact was probably of more importance than any avoidance of syphilis or some related infection. Indeed, it was sometimes said that guardsmen were able to form relationships with women of property, tradesmen's wives, and even (says Mayhew) ladies, who gave the soldiers money.

We shall almost certainly never know the realities of army sex and its results in human terms. Behind entrenched attitudes and official statistics there remains the prostitute or camp follower – the terms are probably interchangeable. Certainly in the nineteenth century, and probably beyond, there were more of them than there were 'amateurs', so that the testimony of one such woman is worth hearing. Henry Mayhew met her near Knightsbridge Barracks, and she told him that she had been a soldier's woman all her life.

> When I was sixteen I went wrong. I'm up'ards of thirty now. I've been fourteen or fifteen years at it. It's one of those things you can't well leave off when you've once took to it. I was born in Chatham. We had a small baker's shop there, and I served the customers and minded the shop. There's lots of soldiers at Chatham, as you know, and they used to look in at the window in passing, and nod and laugh whenever they could catch my eye. I liked to be noticed by the soldiers. At last one young fellow, a recruit, who had not long joined I think, for he told me he hadn't been long at the depot, came in and talked to me. Well, this went on, and things fell out as they always do with girls who go about with men, more especially soldiers, and when the regiment went to Ireland, he gave me a little money that helped me to follow it; and I went about from place to place, time after time, always sticking to the same regiment. My first man got tired of me in a year or two, but that didn't matter. I took up with a sergeant then, which was a cut above a private, and helped me on wonderful. When we were at Dover, there was a militia permanently embodied artillery regiment quartered with us on the western heights, and I got talking to some of the officers, who liked me a bit. I was a — sight prettier than I am now, you may take your dying oath, and they noticed me uncommon; and although I did not altogether cut my old friends, I carried on with these fellows all the time we were there, and made a lot of money, and bought better dresses and some jewellery, that altered me wonderful. One officer offered to keep me if I liked to come and live with him. He said he would take a house for me in the town, and keep a pony carriage if I would consent; but although I saw it would make me rise

A mid-Victorian streetwalker.

in the world, I refused. I was fond of my old associates, and did not like the society of gentlemen; so, when the regiment left Dover, I went with them till I was five and twenty. We were then stationed in London, and I one day saw a private in the Blues with one of my friends, and for the first time in my life I fell in love. He spoke to me, and I immediately accepted his proposals, left my old friends and went to live in a new locality, among strangers; and I've been amongst the Blues ever since, going from one to the other, never keeping to one long, and not particler [sic] as long as I get the needful. I don't get much – very little, hardly enough to live upon. I've done a little needlework in the day-time. I don't now, although I do some washing and mangling now and then to help it out. I don't pay much for my bed-room, only six bob a week, and dear at that. It ain't much of a place. Some of the girls about here live in houses. I don't; I never could abear it. You ain't your own master, and I always liked my freedom. I'm not comfortable exactly; it's a brutal sort of life this. It isn't the sin of it, though, that worries me. I don't dare think of that much, but I do think how happy I might have been if I'd always lived at Chatham, and married as other women do, and had a nice home and children; that's what I want, and when I think of all that, I do cut up. It's enough to drive a woman wild to think that she's given up all chance of it. I feel I'm not respected either. If I have a row with any fellow, he's always the first to taunt me with being what he and his fellows have made me. I don't feel it so much now. I used to at first. One dovetails into all that sort of thing in time, and the edge of your feelings, as I may say, wears off by degrees. That's what it is . . .

Three guardsmen pursue a milliner through St James's Park, 1859. Poverty and exploitation drove many such women to supplement meagre incomes by part-time prostitution.

This passage of autobiography as told to Mayhew seems to me to convey something of the underside of barrack life in mid-Victorian England. It was a shifting, often precarious, world – especially for the women involved – and its transient quality could bring squalor and sharpen anger and personal violence. It was far removed indeed from the glitter of reviews, ceremonial guards, bright uniforms and martial music which make up a more customary image of the army at this period.

In India, where there was a great concentration of British troops, things were rather different. By the middle of the nineteenth century about 40,000 men were stationed there, and after the Mutiny of 1857 the number increased to 60,000. Despite the brave words quoted earlier about sport and athletics as a deterrent to sexual activity, venereal disease was widespread amongst the units scattered through the sub-continent. One of the most important ways in which the problem was tackled was the establishment of 'lal bazars' or regimental brothels, where the women were subject to regular medical examination. To hard-pressed commanding officers worried about the high incidence of sex-related disease amongst their men, such institutions seemed a not unreasonable solution; but Anglican clergymen thought otherwise. In 1834 Thomas Carr, Archdeacon to Bombay, described the system: 'A number of females are kept in buildings in a Bazar called the "Lal Bazar" within the lines of the Regiment and the men go there for the gratification of their passions.' Such places, conceded the Archdeacon, helped to prevent soldiers from contracting venereal disease; but this, he held, was not the point: ' . . . it has pleased Providence to order that sin and misery should be connected, and the arrangement of which I complain is an attempt to make sinning safe.' Carr complained to the Bishop of Calcutta about soldiers who were able to 'indulge their sinful passions, not merely with safety as far as disease is concerned, but with the sanction of their superiors.' Such protests cut very little ice and the lal bazar system prevailed largely because it was supported by senior officers like Major-General S.B. Auchmuty, commanding the Poona Division. 'Where the number of unmarried men', he wrote to the Adjutant-General in 1851, 'is as great as it is in a European cantonment, prostitutes of one class or another are sure to be found in the neighbourhood; their existence is unavoidable, but their actual presence and pursuits need not be so paraded as to shock all sense of public decorum.' The note of reality implicit in such a statement by a divisional commander was echoed down the years by the commanding officers of regiments stationed in India. In May 1861 Lieutenant-Colonel E.R. Priestley of the 42nd Highlanders complained about the existence of unauthorised brothels near his camp, and the assistant surgeon of the unit claimed that 'the regimental prostitutes were free from VD, but of 51 men in hospital, 33 had VD. They must have caught it in the nearby villages.'

Twenty-five years later, in 1886, the officer commanding the 2nd Battalion Cheshire Regiment sent to the Cantonment Magistrate at Ambala a 'Requisition for extra attractive women for the Regimental Bazar (Soldiers)'. The strength of his unit, he wrote in support of his request, was 400. They had six women and required six more – and he asked that they should be 'young and attractive'. In further support of what must have been a fairly unusual request to a magistrate, the officer concerned quoted from a circular which had been issued by the Quarter-master-General a month earlier, in which attention had been drawn to the Commander-in-Chief's concern about the spread of venereal disease among European troops and his anxiety to check it. One method of doing so, said the Q.M.G., Major-General F.E. Chapman, was to have 'a sufficient number of women, to take care that they are sufficiently attractive, to provide them with proper houses . . . ' Such outspoken advocacy of licensed brothels, even in a military document, bordered upon indiscretion. Would any senior staff officer have dared to put such ideas to paper and circulate them in a garrison on the British mainland? I know of none who did so, and VD was rife in the Victorian army stationed at home. India, however, was perceived to be different. Its women – no less than its men – were members of a subject race; they were not white, nor were many of them Christians. In such circumstances, with Britain as the colonial power, the question of double standards simply did not arise. The lal bazar was part of an ordered military environment which kept men free from venereal contamination, and also from what many saw as unsettling contact with the Indian population. It hardly needs to be added that the Military Police, as a matter of course, turned Indian males out of brothels which were used by British soldiers (see Ballhatchet, 1980).

Barrack room scene: soldiers, wives and children. Late eighteenth century.

Inevitably venereal disease remained a problem, and during both world wars, with large numbers of men and women concerned, it became a more pressing one. Methods of treatment improved, and it seems that such disease is no longer the scourge to the army that it once was. In the late 1980s another disease has taken its place: with many troops going to East Africa on training exercises and then being given leave in coastal towns like Mombasa, AIDS has become a major issue. All men proceeding to that part of the world are counselled about the disease and its consequences. At the time of writing it is causing grave concern to the army authorities, as it is indeed to society at large.

Whilst not stamping it out, the attempts to control venereal disease in India were not without success. An ability to come to terms with the inevitable has often characterised the approach of military authority to unofficial contacts between soldiers and women of the countries where men are stationed. In Germany, for example, there was in force in the British zone of occupation after the Second World War a 'non-fraternisation' order forbidding anything but the most formal interchange between victor and vanquished. By the summer of 1946 it was suspended, and contacts between soldiers and German women which had hitherto been covert and subject to disciplinary action against the soldier if discovered became legal. At about the same time the wives and children of regular soldiers began arriving in the Rhine Army – beginning, though no one could foresee this at the time, a tradition of British military families living in Germany which has lasted for more than forty years and still continues.

Such military dependants, living comfortably in houses provided by the army, are a far cry indeed from that small number of wives and children who were allowed to live in barracks with their husbands, a practice which seems to have started towards the end of the 1790s. These families fared very hard indeed, with few facilities. Accommodation for men in the early barracks was poor and rudimentary: wives, with children, inhabited screened-off corners of barrack rooms, or several families would share a room set aside for their use. Sometimes a soldier's rank might entitle him to a room for the exclusive use of his family. In Portman Street Barracks, for instance, as late as the 1850s, a Sergeant-Major, his wife and four children including a girl of fourteen were occupying one room which they used for eating and sleeping; and it was rendered unbearable in hot weather because a drain passed directly beneath it.

Families were well established in barracks by this period. Some time earlier, in fact, they had been the subject of criticism, and one regimental officer, Lieutenant-Colonel A.H. Trevor, was perhaps voicing the feeling of many of his contemporaries when he wrote to *The Naval and Military Gazette* in April 1843:

> . . . these wretched creatures are allowed to crowd into Barracks, with their starving children – some with families of 5, 6, 7 & 8 (I have this last number in the depot) taking up the room, bedding, tables, fires of the men – destroying their comfort, and all attempts at cleanliness – making the Soldiers discontented & driving them to the Canteen or Beer Shop and frequently to Desertion. Soldiers wives, are

Military wedding, late eighteenth century.

generally the greatest nuisances – and I have had more trouble to
control their conduct & behaviour than I can describe – altogether
the system of admitting them into men's rooms is revolting to decency
– and certainly demoralizing – there have been too many inducements
held out for marriage amongst Soldiers and what is the consequence –
the man is starved – his children are naked & starved – and the wife –
she is not to be described – it is a sad case – and to keep up anything
like propriety I am obliged to appear hardhearted & stern – not
allowing a woman of the Regiment to come near me. If she has
anything to say she must make her husband her attorney – I manage
to keep up with the washing according to the families, which I
distributed myself, not leaving it to the Captains of Companies . . .

The Crimean War was the last in which wives accompanied their
husbands on active service. The discontinuance of a time-honoured
practice which senior officers had come to accept in a spirit of resignation
rather than one of enthusiasm was due to several factors. The reforms in
army administration which followed the war took place in a rapidly
changing moral climate. It is worth noting, perhaps, that in the French
army no woman other than those who ran regimental canteens – the
vivandières – went to the Crimea. During hostilities the intervention of

Florence Nightingale, with her advocacy of professional nursing for wounded men, together with the increasing use of Soyer stoves operated by regimental cooks, both went some way to rendering superfluous two of the main duties undertaken by soldiers' wives in the field.

The wives who did accompany their menfolk to the Crimea had a very hard time, and were not always able to be with their husbands. 'When the 95th left Weedon for the Crimea', says the regimental history, 'two soldiers' wives per company went with them, that is twenty in all. But some of them were left at Varna. Only three, Mrs Polley, Mrs Crangle, and Mrs Buller were allowed to go into camp before Sebastopol. The remainder were left on board ship.' At one point during the war some three hundred wives and children were living in conditions of horrifying degradation in the cellars of a Turkish hospital at Scutari which had been taken over. When news of this reached the public in Britain a relief fund for these unfortunate dependants was started. Such tales, together with a pictorial record of this muddled and mismanaged campaign provided by pioneer photographers, gave impetus to the demand for army reform. Many administrative anomalies relating to pay and service were tidied up, and there was a considerable programme of barrack building which now included the erection of permanent quarters for the use of married men and their families. Such accommodation, despite cramped rooms and minimal furniture, marked a real step forward in the official acceptance of married soldiers. The army would now take some responsibility for the welfare and living conditions of their wives and children.

Many of the married quarters built during the nineteenth century remained in use until after the Second World War, when so many barrack complexes were rebuilt and redeveloped. Military estates were constructed where houses not only reflected the rank of the soldier occupant but reflected for everyone the increased standards of hygiene and comfort which are now taken for granted. In 1931 Mrs Irene Burton, wife of Colour Sergeant Burton, Royal Welch Fusiliers, landed at Gibraltar to join her husband whose battalion was stationed there. He was not at the quay to meet her, and she travelled with other wives, in a motor lorry, to her quarters. The home she found awaiting her consisted of one room with a bedroom and a kitchen leading off it. The lavatory was approached through the kitchen; there was no bath, and the only washing facilities consisted of the kitchen sink; everything was filthy and the larder was crawling with ants. Shortly after her arrival a coal ration and NAAFI stores were delivered, and then her husband came – to say only that he could not stay, would get his dinner in the Sergeants' Mess, and what would she have? Irene was rescued by the Sergeant-Major's wife who came in with her two daughters, helped with the unpacking and settling in, then cooked a meal for the four of them. To say the least, this episode reflects a casual attitude to wives on the part of the regiment no less than the husband; but the Royal Welch Fusiliers had something of a reputation in those days for the cavalier treatment of such newcomers. The regiment considered itself, not without some reason, to be very distinguished, and the woman who married into it ought to count herself fortunate . . .

An army family in the 1880s.

Eventually Irene was able to do so, for she moved to a better quarter with a bath and the kitchen (it had a lid which converted it for use as a table) and a boiler for laundry, this latter task performed each week by a Spanish girl who came over from La Linea to work for several British families.

The social activities of the regiment, a regular feature of garrison life, were strictly regulated by the rank of the husband. The private soldier's wife and the sergeant's wife may – like Judy O'Grady and the colonel's lady – have been sisters under the skin, but they did not go to the same social functions within the regiment. At least one case is recorded in recent years of an army marriage where the wife, a serving sergeant, and the husband who was a corporal, had to socialise in separate messes!

This theme of rank was mentioned by a contemporary army wife, married to a corporal, who foresaw that when her husband was promoted to sergeant she would go to mess functions and not to gatherings with wives of corporals and privates. She was frank, too, about the difficulties of being married to a soldier. There were unaccompanied postings, absence on field exercises – in one year, she said, they had spent only five months, inclusive of a period of leave, together. On the other hand it was a secure job. Despite occasional boredom it was, she felt, on the whole not a bad life.

Chapter 5

ON THE MOVE

So 'ark an' 'eed you rookies, which is always grumblin' sore,
There's worser things than marchin' from Umballa to Cawnpore;
An' if your 'eels are blistered an' they feels to 'urt like 'ell
You drop some tallow in your socks an' that will make 'em well,
For it's best foot first . . .

So wrote Rudyard Kipling in a poem entitled 'Route Marchin''. Not for nothing were infantry battalions in the past known as 'marching regiments' or 'the foot', for they marched pretty well everywhere except to foreign stations whither they were conveyed in ships offering minimal facilities, chartered for the purpose. The marching tradition in the army grew out of necessity, and originally it was part of a culture in which for most people walking long distances was taken for granted. There is absolutely nothing inherently improbable in the many fictional accounts of this. In Thomas Hardy's novels, for instance, many characters tramped into and from the county town of Wessex, besides thronging its roads. In *The Old Curiosity Shop*, Little Nell and her grandfather, an old man not in the best of health, left London as pedestrians for a distant and uncertain destination . . . It is hardly surprising, then, that men who joined up before the era of public or personal transport would have seen nothing out of the ordinary in marching long distances.

Although by 1914 trains had long been used for transporting troops overland, marching remained important during the Great War, when considerable distances were covered in this way by units on the Western Front and other theatres of war. Marching, despite 'lorried infantry brigades', continued in the Second World War. The standard training of foot soldiers included a route march, at the pace of three miles an hour, of thirty miles in a day, and also a 'forced march' of twenty miles in five hours. To carry out both successfully, wearing a steel helmet, small pack, belt and ammunition pouches, carrying a rifle and bayonet, was no mean achievement. And today, soldiers in training still march.

The importance of footwear to the soldier at any period cannot be overestimated: the effectiveness of any army would be seriously impaired if boots were not both comfortable and strongly made. Ankle boots, as opposed to riding boots for the cavalry, were not introduced until early in the nineteenth century. Before this, stout shoes had been worn by the infantry. The earliest mention of them that I have found occurs in Captain Bennett Cuthbertson's manual of battalion management published in 1758, and almost certainly it reflected well-established attitudes and practices, besides presaging some of those which were to remain current in the army into the twentieth century:

Two pair of good shoes are indispensably necessary for a Soldier, as he must otherwise be obliged (if depending on one pair) after a wet day's march, to give them a hasty drying by the fire, which not only cracks the leather, but is the certain method of shrinking them in such a manner, as to give the greatest pain and trouble to the wearer: the best shoes will always be found the cheapest, and it will be necessary to strengthen the heels, with some small nails: the toes should be round and flat: the straps full large enough to fill the buckle: and the quarters high, tight and short, for the advantage of the gaiters being fitted well: the Officers commanding companies ought not to permit a pair of shoes to be delivered to a man, until they have examined whether they are comfortable to these directions, else every Soldier will certainly indulge his own particular taste, in the fashion of his shoes, without considering any other advantage: besides two pair of shoes, a Soldier should have a pair of soles and heels in his knapsack, by which means he can never be distressed, should his shoes want mending on the march, as a shoemaker of the Company can always do them, and that with seasoned leather, which might not be the case, was he to take the immediate chance of the country for it.

A soldier removes a comrade's boots, early nineteenth century.

The gaiters mentioned above had been introduced to prevent dirt and gravel from getting into a soldier's shoes. The supply of footwear was taken very seriously indeed, and the Company shoemaker must have been one of the earliest army tradesmen.

Shoes and gaiters were superseded in 1823 by ankle boots and trousers. The boots were issued without eyelet holes, the intention being that they should be pierced to suit the wearer's foot. No distinction was made between right and left feet, and in many regiments it was laid down that boots should be worn on alternate feet on alternate days in order to prevent uneven wear, and to make the boots last longer. In 1843, however, boots were differentiated between right and left feet, and were issued with eyelet holes for the laces. By this time, too, most infantry regiments would have established a shoemaker's shop, the running of which was the responsibility of the unit Quartermaster.

More specialised footwear was developed for certain combat troops during the Second Word War, although many infantrymen continued to wear old-style boots. Today boots have become more comfortable and more weatherproof, the result of continuing research, and in February 1988 a news item carried on the Radio 4 'Today' programme mentioned the introduction of a new kind of boot described as the 'Rolls Royce' of army boots. A week or so later it was announced that the army was developing an official 'trainer' for general issue. The chances are, said an officer working on the project, that most recruits have seldom worn anything else right through their schooldays.

Towards the end of the eighteenth century attempts were made to find ways of moving troops in the British Isles by means other than route marches. In 1796, for instance, the following news item appeared in the *London Chronicle* dated 29 October:

Yesterday an experiment was made in the Park, before his Royal Highness Field Marshal the Duke of York, of a carriage for the rapid conveyance of troops from place to place. It is a light waggon, which

99

Transport waggon in the
early 1820s.

carried fifty men, with their arms, baggage, etc., drawn by six horses
a-breast, harnessed as in a coach, and ridden by two postillions. This
machine is calculated to travel upon an average nearly as fast as a
stage coach: it went quite round the park, carrying its full comple-
ment of men in ten minutes. They are accommodated with seats, one
higher than the other, so constructed that the men's legs are out of
each other's way. The arms, accoutrements, etc., are deposited in a
kind of narrow chest in the centre of the wagon. It met with the
approbation of the military gentlemen present.

Despite such approval, a waggon of this kind seems never to have been
widely used, and indeed may not have gone into general service. Canals
and even rivers, on the other hand, were quite extensively used for troop
transport. In 1806 an entire brigade embarked in barges at Paddington
Basin for the journey to Liverpool. Movement in long boats was not
without its dangers: the *Glocester [sic] Journal* dated 4 March 1799
reported an accident which befell a barge carrying families and invalids of
the Tarbert Fencibles:

A most melancholy sight was witnessed here yesterday, in consequence of the sudden thaw, which caused a great swell in the river
Suir. A part of a regiment of Fencibles, who were on their route from
Clonmell to Waterford, to embark for England, had put their sick,
women, children, and baggage on board a barge to come down the
river, when, just as they came to Carrick bridge, the barge upset, and
every soul on board went down, and out of about seventy only twenty
were saved; not the least assistance could be afforded them. One poor
woman, just as the boat struck, caught hold, as she thought, of her
child, which she held and brought safe to shore; but judge her feelings
when she found it was not her own; the poor creature ran up and
down the river's side in search of her child, but in vain, it perished.
The distress of the poor men, who followed in other barges, and got
ashore about a mile from the town, is better conceived than des-

cribed; some of them seeking their wives, others their children or brothers, and weeping over breathless corpses: one poor man who had lost his wife and two children, in despair plunged himself into the water, but was saved. Those that were saved were put into a house together, and had every assistance given them. Almost all the baggage was lost.

When a unit moved it was customary for its dependants to move with it, and during the eighteenth century when large numbers of soldiers were employed in suppression of smuggling, no less than in the early years of the nineteenth when even larger numbers of men were deployed to deal with industrial unrest in the midland and northern districts of England, movement orders were frequent. Life was made more difficult by the fact that regiments were split up, often at short notice, into detachments for service in different locations.

One unit from the latter period whose movements we can trace in outline over several years is the First Dragoon Guards. They returned from Ireland in 1822 and disembarked at Liverpool. They went straight to Manchester, next to Sheffield, and then back to Liverpool. In the late summer of 1823 the regiment moved to Scotland, where they were stationed successively at Edinburgh and Perth. In the following year they returned to England, and detachments were quartered at Carlisle, Leeds and Newcastle-on-Tyne, whence in 1825 the entire regiment reassembled and marched to Hounslow, to the west of London, to be reviewed by H.R.H. the Duke of York on 28 June. In July they marched to Canterbury, Deal and Shorncliffe, and in the following February two troops were detached for duty in Norwich. A month later the bulk of the regiment went north again to Leeds, Blackburn and Burnley where it was actively engaged in putting down riots. So urgent were the requests of local magistrates for immediate military assistance that some detachments marched, on occasion, between fifty and sixty miles in one day. In 1827 there was a return to Scotland and quarters in Edinburgh, Glasgow, and finally Perth. The following year the First Dragoon Guards went south again to York, Newcastle upon Tyne, Carlisle and Beverley. October 1828 found the regiment in Manchester once more, where they were used in anti-riot duties with detachments active in Macclesfield and Rochdale. A year later the Dragoons went back to Ireland to face more civil unrest.

Such movement of troops between towns, often at short notice, was in no way untypical for regiments which, perforce, carried out duties which in the twentieth century would be undertaken by the civil police. The rapid change of location, together with the fact that regiments all too rarely acted in a concerted manner but rather in scattered detachments of varying size, typifies what John Houlding, a Canadian historian, has called 'the friction of peace'. It must have put a great strain on the administrative machinery of individual units, besides affecting, to a greater or lesser extent, the inner life of the regiment concerned. We have almost everything to learn about how such moves were organised, and their effect upon individual soldiers.

A painting by H.P. Parker in possession of 1st The Queen's Dragoon

OVERLEAF:
The Imperial Adventure. British troops with locally enlisted sepoys on the march in India, 1848. At that time there was no special tropical dress, so the men are dressed as they would be for a review in Hyde Park. Khaki drill uniforms became a general issue in India in 1885. Scarlet was finally superceded by khaki throughout the British army in 1902.

101

Moving station: a baggage cart in the mid-Victorian period. Unless the soldier reclining on a pile of goods is sick, he is disobeying orders by travelling in this fashion.

Guards (the present title of the regiment whose moves were outlined above), showing preparations for leaving Newcastle upon Tyne in 1825, gives some idea of how it must have looked to soldiers and their dependants. Four baggage waggons are piled high, with wives and children either sitting on the baggage or preparing to do so. Officially only the sick were entitled to ride on baggage waggons, but from the picture it appears that women and young children did so as well. A baggage guard would be detailed, and the pace of the waggons on the road would be regulated so that they arrived at the end of a day's march with the regiment. We have, in this picture, a rare glimpse of a scene which was frequently re-enacted in towns where entire regiments or detachments were on the move, before the railway system began to carry an increasing proportion of the troops. Tradition, as always, died hard in the army, and the practice of route marching to a new location survived in some regiments until the turn of the century. In July/August 1845 the 13th Foot landed at Gravesend after twenty-two continuous years of service in India and Burma, and from their port of disembarkation they marched to Walmer, a distance of some fifty miles. In July 1891 the same regiment – since 1881 re-named the Somerset Light Infantry – marched from Aldershot to London to take part in the ceremonies attended upon the visit of the German Emperor; and when their duties were performed they marched back to Aldershot.

By the last few years of the nineteenth century, though, railways were carrying most troops on the move. Special trains or reserved coaches on scheduled services were used. Indeed, one of the recurring images of the Boer War is that of trains packed with soldiers departing for their port of embarkation; and there is, too, the connection of Victoria Station and other main termini during the Great War with the fighting in France and Flanders, the constant arrival of wounded men, soldiers coming on leave or returning from it, others going out to the Western Front for the first time. Outside these stations buses are still living reminders of the old London General Omnibus Company – double-decked, open-topped vehicles which were requisitioned for troop transport in the battle zone.

Regiments ordered overseas, of course, had to go by ship. If weather and wind were favourable, short journeys to the continental ports of Northern France and the Low Countries were bearable; but longer journeys to India, the Far East, the West Indies, North America, Canada and Egypt entailed not just tremendous discomfort and overcrowding but a very serious threat to health as well. Many men died on troopships. In the winter of 1706–1707 an army of 8,200 men, commanded by Earl Rivers, embarked at Torbay for Spain. On arrival at Valencia only 4,500 men came ashore. The rest had died on the way. Charles Dickens in *The Uncommercial Traveller* described the arrival of a troopship, *The Great Tasmania*, at Liverpool in about 1857. It was carrying some two hundred sick and wounded from the Indian Mutiny, and on landing they were taken at once to the workhouse infirmary. 'They had been brought through the rain in carts, it seemed, from the landing-place to the workhouse gate, and had been carried upstairs on the backs of paupers. Their groans and pains during the performance of this glorious pageant had been so distressing as to bring tears to the eyes of spectators . . .' That these men were in so poor a condition on arrival in England hints at their nightmare journey from India.

Conditions remained squalid until well into the twentieth century, as soldiers proceeding to Korea just after the Second World War could testify. The toll of human life was not nearly so great, but the experience on ship, especially for other ranks, was grim. The last occasion on which large numbers of troops and equipment were moved by sea over a long distance was in 1982, when the expeditionary force went to the Falkland Islands. Conditions for all ranks were good – but this foray into the South Atlantic was an exceptional one.

Despite the euphoric tone of a song popular in the Second World War about a troopship leaving Bombay, this kind of transport was never popular with the rank and file. As Private Deane, serving in Queen Anne's army, put it, travelling by sea meant 'labouring under very many inconveniences, having only the bare Deck to lye upon, which hardship caused abundance of our men to bid adieu to this world'. The sheer nastiness of

Life on board a troopship in 1880. Conditions were cramped; accomodation and facilities crowded. The discomfort as the ship moved into the tropics can only be imagined. Unlike most European soldiers, the British soldier spent much of his service abroad, policing the Empire.

life at sea for soldiers in transit was emphasised more than a hundred years later by John Shipp (his autobiography, *Memoirs of the Military Career of John Shipp*, was published in 1843), who described the scene he witnessed on a troopship bound for India as 'truly distressing: soldiers, their wives and children, all lay together in a state of most dreadful sea-sickness, groaning in concert . . . ' Lack of fresh fruit and vegetables caused an outbreak of scurvy among the crew and passengers: 'Scarcely an individual on board escaped the melancholy disorder, and the swollen legs, the gums protruding beyond the lips, attested to the malignancy of the visitation. The dying were burying the dead . . . ' Corpses were thrown overboard and immediately eaten by sharks. When at last landfall was made, Shipp noted with feeling that 'Everyone on board seemed elated with joy.'

Apart from the near-certainty of sickness and the possibility of death, shipwreck was a hazard. The loss of the *Birkenhead*, packed with soldiers and their families, en route for India in 1852 was only one of several disasters. The vessel struck a rock somewhere between Simon's Bay and Port Elizabeth off the coast of South Africa. 'I was asleep below', wrote Private John Smith of The Queen's (Second) Royal Regiment of Foot, 'when I was aroused by a tremendous crash. I at once realised that something serious was amiss, and calling to my mate, a Romford man, I told him I thought we must be ashore. We ran up on deck with the rest, and afterwards I stood at the gangway and assisted to hand the women and children into the boats.' The men all stood back until they had got safely away; but there was no 'falling in' on deck. Smith was in the water for fourteen hours before he drifted to the shore, and it was two days later before he found his way to the house of a settler, an ex-officer, Captain Smales, who gave Smith and several other survivors something to eat. After active service in Africa he returned to England, left the army in 1861, and served with the Great Eastern Railway for thirty-seven years. Another survivor from the *Birkenhead* was Corporal John O'Neil of the 91st Regiment, who had been on board for only half an hour before the ship struck the rock and sank within twenty minutes. He described how all the women and children were helped off the ship, and there were no casualties amongst them. The soldiers were lined up on deck: 'The water rose as the ship was sinking. Before we left her we were up to our necks in water on the top deck . . . There was a lurch and a plunge, and all was over. I found myself in the water and struck out for the shore.' O'Neil paid tribute to the gallantry of Major Wright of his regiment, of whom he said: 'If it had not been for him all hands would have been lost, women and children and all.' Major Wright also survived.

Other tragedies took place nearer home. In 1955 the East Lancashire Regiment (now incorporated in the Queen's Lancashire Regiment) paid to restore a monument in the burial ground of Christ Church (Drumcannon) at Tramore in Waterford, Eire, commemorating a disaster suffered by their forebears, the 59th Foot. The *Seahorse* transport was wrecked in the bay on 30 January 1816 with considerable loss of life: twelve officers, two hundred and sixty-four other ranks, seventy-one women and children and sixteen of the ship's crew were drowned. Only four officers and twenty-six men survived the accident, which took place within a mile of the Irish shore.

It is not until well into the eighteenth century that we have more than the sketchiest of material about early troopships. On long journeys men were normally carried on transports at the rate of one man to every two tons of the ship's measured tonnage. This meant that a ship of five hundred tons would carrry two hundred and fifty men. On briefer journeys, or when there was a shortage of transport, the rate might exceed one ton per man. On one crossing from Stade in Germany to Portsmouth in 1778, six hundred and seventy-four German mercenary troops en route for British service in America were squeezed into a transport of five hundred and twenty-six tons. General Fawcett, who was in charge of mustering the Germans, admitted 'they will be a little crowded . . . there being however no remedy for these inconveniences . . . they must admit to them till they get to Portsmouth.' Overcrowding on transports was quite common – on one voyage no less than twenty-two Hanoverians died on the passage from Germany to Spithead.

Most of the transports used during the American Revolution were armed merchantmen of two hundred to three hundred tons, and the first description of quarters for the men below deck which is known to me dates from this period:

> The men were packed like herring. A tall man could not stand upright between decks, nor sit up straight in his berth. To every such berth six men were allotted, but as there were room for only four, the last two had to squeeze in as best they might. Thus the men lay in what boys call 'spoon fashion', and when they tired on one side, the man on the right would call 'about face', and the file would turn over at once; then, when they were tired again, the man on the left would give the same order, and they would turn back to the first side. – E.J. Lowell, *The Hessians and other German Auxiliaries of Great Britain in the Revolutionary War*, 1884.

Sometimes in a heavy sea the berths would collapse when the ship rolled. The bedding was scanty, consisting of a straw-filled mattress, a pillow, blanket and coverlet; but the quality of these items, often because of dishonesty on the parts of contractors supplying them, was likely to be inferior. Regimental commanders would sometimes permit men embarking for a long voyage to take part of their barrack bedding with them.

Food on board was poor. Except for troops proceeding to the East Indies, to India or just before carrying out amphibious operations in North America, soldiers on board received two-thirds of usual rations – defined as six soldiers having the same issue of food as four seamen. The greatest defect of maritime rations was the lack of Vitamin C, present in fresh fruit and vegetables, and lack of this could result in an outbreak of scurvy. There was a daily issue of rum, but no other spirits were permitted. Life on a transport during a long voyage, wherever it was bound, was tedious, and made possible only by adherence to a strict routine. Every morning cabins and berths were cleared and probably disinfected with vinegar. Weather permitting, all bedding was brought on deck and aired. In some regiments the men were made to wash themslves daily – not always an easy task because washing and toilet facilities for large numbers were sketchy in the extreme. No gambling was allowed, and smoking below deck was forbidden. In the early evening all lights and fires were extinguished to minimise the danger of fire on board, and in some regiments squads of officers and men kept watches during the night hours. If a ship entered port en route for its final destination, no officer or soldier was allowed ashore without permission. The routine outlined was probably not quite so bleak in practice as it sounds, and was designed to preserve both health and military discipline during a period of inactivity when most kinds of training were impractical, facilities for exercise virtually non-existent, and boredom endemic.

Despite such precautions as were taken, men did die on lengthy trooping voyages, and many more fell ill. A convoy which landed in New York at the end of August 1779 lost one hundred men out of 3,868 other ranks; and 795 of these men were sick with what was described as 'a malignant jail fever' which infected 6,000 men of th garrison shortly after the drafts from Europe had landed. Between October 1776 and February 1780 fourteen regiments totalling 8,437 men were sent to the West Indies, and 932 of them died at sea. The average death rate amongst these units was eleven per cent of the men who embarked, while the average mortality on the way to North America was slightly smaller at eight per cent. Figures like these go a long way towards explaining why sea transport has been traditionally looked upon with disfavour by the army.

The prevalence of sickness on troopships led Sir Ralph Abercromby to suggest in 1795 that for every one hundred men on board the following emergency stores should be made available.

One dozen of Port Wine	
Portable Soup	6 lbs.
Pearl Barley	28 lbs.
Rice	28 lbs.
Moist Sugar	28 lbs.
Soap	6 lbs.

The suggestion was put into operation at once when an expedition to the West Indies led by Sir Ralph and Admiral Hugh Christian was preparing to sail from Portsmouth and Cork in October of that year. Further precautions against the spread of sickness on board were also taken: a hospital ship to which sick men could be transferred accompanied the convoy, and the men's living quarters below deck were whitewashed once a month. These measures for preventing infection became standard practice, and were to some extent effective, indicating at least that the military authorities in London were no longer so prepared to accept the losses through sickness of trained soldiers when some fairly simple precautions could be taken to maintain general health in transit. Problems of overcrowding, poor diet, inadequate facilities and boredom were not done away with, but the insistence upon cleanliness and strict routine, and

upon exercise wherever possible, did much to reduce the mortality rate. During the wars against revolutionary France over 135,000 soldiers were transported successfully to theatres of war overseas; and during the nineteenth century further improvements in transporting large numbers of men were made, especially with the coming of the steamship where accommodation could be more spacious and journey times shorter.

Private E.C. Moffett of the Scots Guards went to South Africa in 1900, and described what life on the troopship was like in his autobiography, *With the Eighth Division*, published in 1903:

> The troop deck at night is a weird picture, and it is impossible to move about save on one's hands and knees – the hammocks swing so near the deck. The deck itself is covered with sleeping forms in more or less picturesque attitudes.
>
> Beyond the usual duties of swabbing, mess-work, guards, pickets and fatigues, there is little else to record.
>
> After a couple of parades a day, comprising physical drill and kit inspection, the troops are at liberty to spend their time as they wish. To some, the monotony of the voyage weighs disagreeably, whilst others divide their time between reading and gazing at the wonders of the deep . . .

There were also, he says, illegal games of crown and anchor (today's bingo) which occupied many of the men, with someone always keeping a

Members of the Royal Artillery regiment embarking for foreign service in the 1930s.

109

look out for the Provost Sergeant on his rounds; and there was a dry canteen, although using it entailed a great deal of queueing with 1,300 men on board. Moffett was critical about the food. There were three meals a day, and breakfast consisted of very inferior coffee, dry bread and porridge. Dinner served at midday was mainly soup or stew; and tea, last meal of the day, comprised tea and dry bread. By any standards this was a poor diet, but at least the meals were regular and it was certainly no worse than the food which many working-class families at home had to subsist on – and their pattern of eating was often haphazard.

Today long-distance trooping on a large scale is a thing of the past. The bulk of soldiers permanently stationed abroad are in Germany, which is easily reached. For longer distances aeroplanes transport comparatively small numbers of men and equipment – a method which is convenient, quick and comfortable, but almost certainly, because troop movement is now institutionalised, much less interesting to the historian!

Finally, there was transport by train. Thousands upon thousands of British soldiers stationed in India over the years must have undergone long, tedious journeys across the sub-continent. Rudyard Kipling described one of the recurring discomforts in his poem 'Gunga Din':

> . . . the sweatin' troop-train lay
> In a sidin' through the day
> Where the 'eat would make your bloomin' eyebrows crawl . . .

Railways were extensively used in the Great War, and immediately after the Second World War the army organised a series of trans-European trains which began at the great railhead in Calais and travelled to Berlin in one direction and to Trieste in another. For many travelling west, German rolling stock was used and one travelled either 'hard and clean' or 'soft and dirty'. The former meant wooden bench-type seats that were uninfected by the lice and assorted insects which lurked in the ruined upholstery of the softer seating. NAAFI, mentioned in a previous chapter, provided a good canteen service on the long-distance trains, while food other than 'char and wads' (as the army called tea and cakes) was served in a series of Rail Feeding Points run by the Army Catering Corps. The procedure was that a scheduled military train halted at the location of a feeding point and a de-training ritual began. Nobody left the train until bidden to do so by the impersonal voice of a loudspeaker. There might be a delay, or if the train was late the operation would begin at once. Officers went first, then warrant officers and sergeants, and then the rank and file. Each group went to a separate mess where they were served with a hot meal. One quirk of the system was that the train which started out from Berlin arrived after a long journey, picking up passengers at Münster and Osnabruck, pulled into the Rail Feeding Point at Krefeld regularly at around three in the morning – and its largely somnolent group of passengers was invited to partake of a full meal.

In Britain during the Second World War, hanging about on railway stations waiting for a train or connection became almost a way of life for many soldiers. Even at night or in the small hours on quite unimportant

stations there would be a group of soldiers on the dimly lit platform surrounded by their arms and equipment, dozing on seats or hunched over kitbags, waiting . . . Sometimes a non-stopping train would bump slowly through the station – from which all place-name signs had long since been removed in order, it was said, to confuse enemy parachutists; and invariably someone would shout an enquiry from a carriage as to where they were. Some barely wakeful soldier would detach himself from the group on the platform and reply 'Southwick, mate', or wherever it was. The enquirer probably realised that he was none the wiser. Southwick? Where the hell was that? Such was the tedium of travel in crowded, half-lit carriages through the night, or waiting about on gloomy stations, that these exchanges seemed a brief though welcome diversion of the kind that an artist like Bruce Bairnsfather might have illustrated.

Despite the thousands – probably millions – of miles travelled by the British army in trains on several continents, descriptions of such journeys are hard to find at any period. We know, for example, that during the Great War the station at Poperinge was regarded with ambivalent feelings by Allied troops serving in the Ypres Salient. On the one hand it was the place from which men left to go on leave: on the other it was frequently shelled by German artillery. There are the old jokes about the equivalent numbers of men and horses who could occupy a railway truck . . . Rifleman Aubrey Smith of the London Rifle Brigade, driver in the transport section, described in his book *Four Years on the Western Front*, 1987 (1922), an overnight journey made by rail in November 1917:

Victoria Station, 1915. Troops returning from leave to rejoin their units in the British Expeditionary Force in France and Flanders.

111

A lull in the battle for Amiens, 1918. Two privates from the 10th Londons sit amidst battlefield debris near a captured German machine gun.

affect the futility of settling human affairs by such crude means.

The experience of being in action – the role of broadcasting in modern warfare notwithstanding – is necessarily written about retrospectively, hours, day or even years after the event, and thus the writer's angle of vision is important. Any battle will be seen in very different terms by those who plan it and those who fight it. The Third Battle of Ypres in 1917, for example, was seen in one way by the Commander-in-Chief, Sir Douglas Haig, but in quite another by a medical officer just behind the lines tending the wounded, and differently again by an infantry private lying in the mud under shell fire on Pilckhem Ridge. Because officers have generally been better educated and more articulate than their men, they have been better able to write in books, journals and letters about active service. This is particularly true of the Peninsular War, the Crimean War and the Great War, but holds good for most campaigns in which the British army has been involved. A consequence of this is that we have tended to see action through the eyes of officers. As T.E. Lawrence put it in *The Seven Pillars of Wisdom*, it is 'the unnamed rank and file who miss their share of credit...' Only rarely have we seen the army in battle through the eyes of other ranks. Yet to know what they saw and how they felt is vital, for they have always formed the largest element in every army.

One of the most moving and authentic testimonies to what it was like to be a young soldier in the Great War was written nearly fifty years later (in the *Sunday Times*, 8 March 1964) by an anonymous rifleman who served with the King's Royal Rifle Corps:

I have been going over in my mind all the different things that happened at Ypres and on the Somme. At High Wood on September 9, 1916, we went into action 1,100 strong, and at the end of the day only 110 were standing up with just one officer, a young second lieutenant, and he was crying: I can remember that roll call now. I can remember embarking at Southampton and landing at Le Havre, with Union Jacks on our packs and marching up to Harfleur eager to get in before it was over. There were sixty-six in my draft for the K.R.R. and I was the only one left after three weeks. We went into the salient at Ypres and Jerry came over the same night. I still think of the first bomb I ever threw. I forgot to take the pin out , but that seemed to do me good for I pulled myself together and did my bit. And to think that after it was over, all they could think of was tossing up for sides for the next war.

British infantry going into action during one of the engagements collectively known as the Battle of the Somme, summer-autumn 1916. The steel helmets they are wearing had been introduced in March.

Testimony of this quality, it has to be said, is unusual. As we go further back in time we find a tendency to concentrate upon events rather than feelings, although the implicit attitudes of the writers are usually of interest. Henry Foster served as a sergeant with a City of London regiment in the Parliamentary forces during the early years of the Civil War, and he described an action which took place near Reading. Royalist cavalry fell upon a Parliamentary column in a narrow lane, causing their cavalry to flee. Although some of the infantry were trampled underfoot, the main force resisted the Royalist onslaught:

We fired ten or twelve drakes [small cannon] at the enemy, but they came upon us very fiercely, having their foot on the other side of the hedges; many of our wagons were overthrowne and broken: others cut their traces and horse harnesse, and run away with their horses,

115

leaving their wagons and carriages behind them: our foot fired upon
the enemy's horse very bravely, and slew many of them; some report
above one hundred and not ten of ours: some that we took prisoners
our men were so enraged at them that they knocked out their brains
with the butt end of their muskets. In this great distraction and rout a
wagon of powder lying in the way overthrowne, some spark of fire or
match fell among it, which did much hurt; seven men burnt and two
kill'd: the enemy had got two of our drakes in the rear, had not our
foot played the man and recovered them again: this was about four or
five o'clock at night; many of our men lost their horses, and other
things which they three away in haste . . . – H. Foster, Quondam
Sergeant, *A True and Exact Relation of the Marchings of the Two
Regiments of the Trained Bands of the City of London . . .*, 1643.

More than a century later Samuel Hutton of the 12th Foot wrote with
engaging frankness about being on active service during the Seven Years
War. 'I have been in many engagements, but in no general battle. At the
time of the battle of Minden I was a prisoner, and in a French hospital, so
ill that I could not crawl out of bed.' Describing an attack in which he took
part on Brucker's mill, held by the French, he wrote that 'the oldest
soldiers never saw so severe a cannonade'. The outcome of this attack was
indecisive.

After the battle of Vimiero in 1808 Rifleman Harris tells, in his
Recollections first published in 1848, how he 'strolled about the field in
order to see if there was anything to be found worth picking up amongst
the dead.' He exchanged his own shoes for those of a dead officer, but
while he was doing this a shot was fired at him. 'The dead and the dying
lay thickly all around', and he was unable to make out who had fired. As
he completed the exchange another shot rang out. This time Harris was
ready and saw a French light infantry man some way off. He fired at once
and 'instantly knocked him over'. Still unruffled, Harris quenched his
thirst from his water bottle (which he referred to as a calabash), and
turned over the body. An officer of the 60th Regiment came up to him:

'What! Looking for money, my lad', said he, 'Eh?' 'I am sir', I
answered; 'But I cannot discover where this fellow has hid his hoard.'
'You knocked him over, my man', he said, 'in good style, and deserve
something for the shot. Here,' he continued, stooping down and
feeling in the lining of the Frenchman's coat, 'this is the place where
these rascals generally carry their coin. Rip up the lining of his coat,
and then search in his stock. I seem to know them better than you do.'

Harris did so, and found some money. While he was counting it he heard
the bugler of his regiment sounding call, so 'I touched my cap to the officer
and turned towards them.'

In the first decades of the nineteenth century the French were not the
only enemy. A considerable body of troops were stationed at home to deal
with social unrest in northern and midland England. The Luddites were
perceived by the government to be an especial menace, and after an
outbreak of machine breaking around Nottingham in November 1811, so
the nineteenth-century historian Frank Peel tells us, 'A considerable force
of cavalry and infantry was then sent to Nottingham.' One of the cavalry
troopers serving with the 15th Hussars, known to posterity only as

'Chelsea Pensioner', described in his *Jottings from my Sabretasche* (1847) what active duty entailed in those circumstances. It is the only such account I have found; if soldiers wrote at all, it was about the more acceptable Empire campaigns. The 'Pensioner' was one of a mounted detachment quartered in Nottingham which had to suppress a riot:

> Out we were turned, and proceeded at a rattling pace towards the scene of uproar. The mere sounds emitted from the clattering of the horses' feet upon the pavement, followed by shouts of 'the Sodgers are coming', caused instant consternation and dispersion. The exception comprised some numbers of the softer sex; who, with arms akimbo and clenched fists stuck upon their hips, faced and dared us to ride 'over women' claiming the privilege of the petticoat to abuse us.

In faraway India, Corporal Ryder of the 32nd Foot took part, in 1849, in the Battle of Gujerat, which started at six in the morning:

> A little before four a.m. . . . the orderly sergeant came to tell the corporals to go and see the rations drawn, and get them cooked immediately. This order had not been given many minutes before another came, for us to strike camp and pack our baggage . . . as quickly as possible . . . We had just made fires, and got our frying pans on, and our baggage was not packed, nor the camp struck, when the well-known sound of the bugle was heard, ringing through the camp, for us to stand to arms. All was now confusion: we got a dram of grog served out per man and a pound of bread for every two comrades. Our accoutrements were soon upon us and our muskets in our hands.

The men went into action feeling hungry. Nineteen regiments, including seventeen Indian ones, faced a brave and determined Sikh force which was resisting British rule. The battle went against the Sikhs and they suffered heavy casualties: by four in the afternoon they were in full retreat and the town of Gujerat was stormed. Ascendancy over the Sikhs was established. Losses on the British side were small: Ryder's regiment, for example, lost one man killed, with one officer and four men wounded. In the evening, when it was all over, the commanding general Lord Gough rode along the ranks of his victorious troops, and he was, Ryder tells us quite without irony, 'very full of jokes'.

One of the most celebrated military actions of the entire nineteenth century was the charge of the Light Brigade at the Battle of Balaclava in 1854. A trooper of the 17th Lancers, J.W. Wightman, recalls it in an article published in *The Nineteenth Century* in May 1890. He described in graphic terms how the men riding near him, and their horses, became casualties. Almost apologetically he says: 'My narrative may seem barren of incidents, but amid the crash of shells and the whistle of bullets, the cheers and the dying cries of comrades, the sense of personal danger, the pain of wounds, and the consuming passion to reach an enemy, he must be an exceptional man who is cool enough and curious enough to be looking about him for what painters call "local colour".' Wightman, with eleven comrades from the 17th, was taken prisoner – a captivity from which only he and two others returned. A few days after rejoining their regiment they were courtmartialled on charges of being absent without leave for twelve months! They were, of course, acquitted, and Wightman went on to see action in the Indian Mutiny. 'Tough scenes', he called them – but he does not enlarge upon them.

George Gilham enlisted in the 2nd Battalion The Rifle Brigade in 1870, and four years later he was in West Africa taking part in the Ashanti campaign. When his regiment landed at Cape Coast Castle on 1 January 1874, pipes and tobacco were issued to the men in the hope that smoking would reduce the risk of catching tropical diseases. At the end of the month the main engagement was fought at Amoaful. Skirmishers advancing into the forest came under enemy fire – the Africans were armed with flintlock muskets – and fell back, leaving the main body of British troops to advance. Gilham describes what happened. The order was given:

> 'Chinstraps down, open out, and push on through the jungle.' I was one of the leading four of the front company, and as our skirmishers came in I noticed one with the bones of his arm broken by slugs from the enemy's muskets. We cut our way right and left into the jungle with our cutlasses, lying down in the underwood, standing behind trees for cover, pegging in where we could, and forming a semi-circle to the front; but the foliage was so dense that it was like being in a net, and the further we went the thicker it seemed to get, so that I don't believe we advanced a hundred yards during the whole fight.

There are other details in Gilham's narrative: a sick tent in the rear hastily erected by the Royal Engineers, to which the wounded were taken; rockets and a small field gun used effectively against the Africans; an abortive attack made on the British sick and baggage; and eventually, with their superior fire power, the army was victorious. Sir Garnet Wolseley refused an Ashanti request for a few days' truce because he wanted to end the fighting before tropical rains broke. He took the local capital, Kumasi , and blew up the royal palace on 6 February, and then he and his men returned to the coast in half the time it had taken them to advance inland, burning villages as they went. By 26 March Gilham arrived back in Portsmouth, and four days later his battalion was reviewed by Queen Victoria at Windsor. The Ashanti campaign had been one of the briefest of the so-called 'little wars' of colonial conquest in which so many native peoples were killed defending their homelands, and which at the time did so much to underpin the now discredited myths of white supremacy and European hegemony.

We have remnants of other rank memoirs, journals and letters which offer fascinating insights into what active service in the past was like; and the pictures are not always painful. Private Harbottle, serving in South Africa with the 2nd Northumberland Fusiliers wrote home almost euphorically in September 1900: 'We lead a sort of Gipsey life and when the weather is fine it is most enjoyable . . . ' Nevertheless it was not until the Great War of 1914–1918 that we really have a flood of material describing for posterity the experiences of the rank and file soldier in time of war. There are good reasons why this should be so. Following the Education Act of 1870 the ability to read and write was more widely

Men of Codrington's Brigade (23rd Royal Welch Fusiliers) go into action at the Battle of the Alma, in the Crimea.

spread throughout society than it had ever been. A cheap letter post and concessions for men serving abroad meant an increase in letter writing. Letters from men at the front, despite a strict military censorship, were often kept in families, and in many cases formed the basis of accounts which appeared long after the war. Even where it was not possible to write about details, the mere existence of something written at the time would often serve to jog the memory. It is also true that many educated men, preferring not to be commissioned, served in the ranks. The historian R.H. Tawney, for example, served as a corporal, and a schoolmaster linguist I knew many years ago at Varndean, Cecil Pannet, served in the A.S.C. in the same rank. He let slip in a private conversation one day that while he was stationed in Macedonia he had taught himself a working knowledge of the Russian language in a fortnight. Not everyone, of course, had this ability, but I am suggesting that there were many educated men serving in the ranks throughout the army, and this gave a decisive twist to contemporary writing about the Great War. Much of it is extremely good.

What we are looking for are details of men's daily lives at the front, and how they regarded the war, authority, and the regulations which bounded their lives. Among the many accounts the following extracts are illuminating in various ways. Rifleman Aubrey Smith of the London Rifle Brigade described life in Ploegsteert Wood on the Western Front in March and April 1915:

> One day was very much like another in the Wood and there was little
> time for sleep, with one thing and another. Sandbag-filling parties,

119

ABOVE:
Private Robert Perham, Royal Sussex Regiment. He was one of many under-age young men who volunteered for the army in the earlier part of the Great War. He enlisted in 1915 when he was sixteen, and was killed the next year during the Somme battles.

RIGHT:
Letter from Regimental Records to Private Perham's mother, accompanying the British War Medal 1914–19 and the Victory Medal which were posthumously awarded to her son.

Record Office,
Hounslow

Madam,

I am directed to transmit to you the accompanying British War Medal 14-19 Victory Medal which would have been conferred upon the late No. S.A. 2991 Private robert Charles Perham ROYAL SUSSEX REGIMENT had he lived, in memory of his services with the British Forces during the Great War.

In forwarding the Decoration I am commanded by the King to assure you of His Majesty's high appreciation of the services rendered.

I am to request that you will be so good as to acknowledge the receipt of the Decoration on the attached form.

Mrs. E. Perham
Lower Eastwood Farm
Ifield
Crawley
Sussex

I am, Madam,
Your obedient Servant,

Colonel for Records.

water-carrying parties, wood-carrying parties, meals to cook, rifle-cleaning, and the incessant sentry-duty occupied our time, by day and by night. Heightening the barricade, listening patrol and building block-houses made an occasional change of work.

Smith, whose long and excellent book *Four Years on the Western Front* was reissued by the London Stamp Exchange in 1987, sixty-five years after its original appearance, contains many authentic descriptions of an infantryman's life. Blankets, for example, were withdrawn from men in active units in the spring of each year and reissued in the autumn. In 1916 the spring was cold and wet:

> Just after our arrival the Army called in *all* blankets, this order being followed by a succession of cold nights . . . This collection of blankets every May and redistribution in October became an annual pastime. Red-tape ordained their removal according to the calendar, not to fluctuations in temperature. The Army said it must not, and could not, be cold before October, and – officially – it was not. The troops could therefore never remove their clothes at nights, even when temporarily resting behind the firing line . . .

It was little wonder that many men regarded 'red-tape' with considerable suspicion. 'There is', wrote an anonymous private soldier, 'an unfriendliness about the military authorities.' The same man said that 'One's war seems to have been against the authorities, the elements, and circumstances, not against the Germans. It is only the tiniest exaggeration to say that I have never heard an English soldier speak ill of a German. We referred to the enemy, almost affectionately, as "Jerry".' The man who wrote this was no malcontent, and went on to become a non-commissioned officer and later to take a commission. The point of view he expressed was not, I think, uncommon. J.B. Priestley in his autobiographical book *Margin Released* confirms that such opinions were held by men in the ranks.

Too much, though, should not be made of the soldier's propensity for grousing. In the face of appalling conditions and very heavy casualties, especially during the 3rd Battle of Ypres in 1917, the morale of the British did not break. Are we to ascribe this to what any soldier would simply regard as 'bloodymindedness'? Consider the reactions of an eighteen-year-old private soldier of the Royal Welch Fusiliers during the battle mentioned above:

> Can I ever forget the fearful journey over the mud-flats towards Passchendaele Ridge? Miles around, nothing but stark desolation met the eye. The poor earth, blasted and pitted with countless shell-holes, seemed to cry out in its agony. Those foul, evil-smelling craters, filled with stagnant water, were as much to be feared going up the line, as the shrapnel shells Jerry sent over – for those duckboard tracks were well 'taped'. To slip into a crater meant death by suffocation. We had to pass one poor fellow who had met such an end; he served as a kind of land-mark, a grim reminder to those going up the line.

No sign here of anger, hatred or even self-pity, but it is worth pointing out that the whole passage, with the alteration of just one word, might so easily have been written by somebody in the opposing army.

Some of the great events of the war are recalled by men who took part in them in ways which enhance our understanding of what went on. The capture of Jerusalem in December 1917 by forces commanded by General Allenby was one. What we may perhaps too easily overlook is the fact that its fall was the climax of a brilliant campaign fought by Allenby's men over the preceding months. A sergeant with the 2/13th London Regiment recalled not so much the dangers as the discomforts of fighting in the Holy Land. After an engagement with the Turks at Deir Yesin he wrote:

> . . . the brigade spent a most miserable and uneasy night on the exposed hills, without rations, fires or bivouacs, while the keen wind searched through light summer clothing.
> Men paced up and down to keep warm, or crept beneath the shelter of heaps of stones. Many fell asleep from exhaustion and had to be roused because of the danger of frost-bite. It was a terrible experience for the wounded, some of whom must have succumbed to exposure, although the medical orderlies worked hard to bring them in.

With this quotation from an infantry sergeant in 1917, we approach the end of what might be termed the heroic age of individual reportage. In future wars it was, increasingly, professional communicators who brought to the public much less personal, though often extremely vivid,

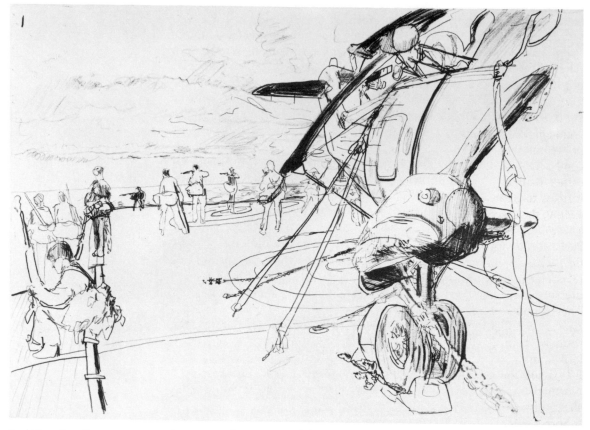

2nd Battalion Scots Guards, live firing from the flight deck of the QE2 during the Falklands conflict, May 1982, drawn by Linda Kitson.

images and accounts of the experience of war. In their task they have been greatly helped by the cine-camera, a technical device that the army was quick to exploit, particularly during the Second World War, with admirable results. A training film like 'Name, Rank and Number', for instance, is still worth seeing for its many insights into army life. Radio, too, played an important part, and there was a new kind of pictorial journalism exemplified at its best in *Picture Post*, a weekly magazine in which short articles accompanied by extremely well-captioned photographs of an unusually high standard conveyed to the public some of the tasks on which the army and its men were engaged. After the war, the development of television has meant that the camera can accompany a British infantryman on patrol in the streets of Belfast. Such immediacy may, in the short view, have led to a serious undervaluing of soldiers' memoirs; but if we recall for a moment the soldier quoted earlier in this chapter who remembered the Somme after nearly fifty years, then I think we may feel that the written memory, however brief, is still uniquely valuable and moving.

Chapter 7

SICK AND WOUNDED

Even in the days before King Charles II established a standing army in 1660, doctors – or surgeons, as they were termed – served with the regiments of the army. They probably wore some kind of distinguishing badge, and appear to have been treated by opposing sides as non-combatants, and perhaps enjoyed privileges that were defined by custom rather than by regulation, often permitted to enter a hostile camp or fortress to treat the wounded men of their own side. If captured by the enemy, they seem rarely to have been retained as prisoners. In 1644, for example , Henry Johnson wrote as surgeon to the King's forces to the Parliamentary governor of Newport Pagnell, requesting that his apprentice, who had been captured in a skirmish near Kidlington, should be released. 'It is well known', wrote Johnson, 'how careful I have been in dressing your wounded men whensoever they have fallen into our hands. Therefore if you will give him a speedy release and safe pass to Oxford, I am very confident that the favour shall not pass without recompense.' The result of this appeal is not known, but clearly the doctors and others who looked after wounded men saw it as their duty to be even-handed with friend and foe. Mrs Hutchinson, wife of the Parliamentary governor of Nottingham, bound up the wounds of soldiers on both sides, doing 'what she thought was her duty in humanity to them, as fellow creatures . . . '

Sometimes at this period the army called in civilian doctors who, unlike their regimental counterparts, would require payment for tending the wounded. The bill submitted by one of them, George Blagrave, in 1645 included the following:

John Cox, I cut in his hand and a very soare wound in his arm	£1. 0. 0.
John Bullock of Capt. Barton's, a very sore cut in the fore-part of his head, which caused a peece of his skull the breadth of a half crowne peece to (be) taken forth, allsoe a very sore cut over his hand	£1. 10. 0. (£1.50)
Richard Hudson, taken prisoner at Ashby, having a sore cut in the shoulder, was sent to be dressed by the governour's command	£0. 6. 8. (about 33p)
One John Curson, a Scotsman, Quartermaster, a very sore wound in the head	£1. 0. 0.

When a soldier was admitted to hospital a certain proportion of his pay was stopped during his sojourn there in order to defray the cost of drugs and nursing. In Heriot's Hospital in 1653, for example, foot soldiers were charged one shilling (5p) per week, while the cost for a cavalryman was

Care for sick and wounded men in India, early 1850s.

twice as much. It was generally accepted that women made the best nurses, and at the Savoy Hospital in London it was ordered that they should 'be chosen from the widows of soldiers, so far as fit ones can be found.' In this particular hospital there were thirty-nine nurses to about three hundred and fifty patients. In Dublin, on the other hand, one nurse was allowed for every ten sick or wounded men, while in Edinburgh the ratio was one nurse to every five 'weak men'. It seems to have been a general rule throughout the Parliamentary army that if a soldier married his nurse then she lost her job. Presumably in hospitals run by the Royalist army conditions and regulations would have been much the same.

Medical men on both sides would have relied heavily upon John Woodall, *The Surgeon's Mate*, a very popular handbook first published in 1617, which went through four editions before 1655 and which provided practical guidance in the treatment of wounds. In a biography published in 1891 of Richard Wiseman, a Royalist surgeon who served in the West of England in the mid-1640s, there are some interesting details of how wounded men were treated. It is also worth noting that in 1652 some three hundred and twenty convalescent soldiers were sent from London to Bath 'for the recovery of their limbs and perfecting their cure' by means of the waters.

What were conditions in hospital like? What did men think of the treatment they received? Who were the nurses and orderlies? We have no way of knowing, because no one, so far as I am aware, has left any testimony behind. Rank and file in seventeenth-century armies were largely – though not always – inarticulate, and all that have come down to us are occasional names. We can, therefore, only generalise about the treatment of sick and wounded soldiers from what is known about general conditions of the time; and these would lead one to suggest that standards of care, sanitation and hygiene were not high. What is more, they did not improve as the years went by. 'The wounded men . . . are intirely neglected', wrote a surgeon's mate in 1711.

Throughout the eighteenth century the system of regimental surgeons, with each one appointed by the commanding officer, remained in force. It was not until the end of this period that it was necessary for a doctor to be professionally qualified to obtain employment in the army. It is said that in 1745 a private soldier was taken out of the ranks and appointed to the medical charge of his unit simply because he was reputed to have been 'bred a surgeon'. Tobias Smollett, the novelist, sailed as a qualified ship's surgeon with the expedition sent to Carthagena, West Indies, in the spring of 1741, and wrote about the plight of the sick and wounded soldiers who were:

> . . . next day sent on board of the transports and vessels called hospital ships, where they languished in want of every necessary comfort and accomodation. They were destitute of surgeons, nurses, cooks, and proper provision; they were pent up between decks in small vessels, where they had no room to sit upright . . .

All they could do, said Smollett, was to wash down the infected wounds and sores with their allowance of brandy. As a doctor, what he has to say about the fate of casualties is of special interest. He stressed the lack of qualified army doctors, and said that naval surgeons were not sent to aid the wounded troops, though several applied to do so. Smollett blamed rancour and jealousy amongst high-ranking officers for this sorry state of affairs.

The attitude of authority to the health of soldiers was summed up in an official minute of 1758, which laid down that 'if men are sick they must be put under stoppages [i.e. of pay] to pay for their cures.' Although each unit had its own surgeon, during the eighteenth century many regiments serving at home were broken up into small detachments in widely separated localities, often far from regimental headquarters where the surgeon would normally be. Sick soldiers, therefore, might have to call upon the services of a civilian doctor; and he, in his turn, would make a claim upon the army in respect of any treatment given. In 1746 one doctor put in a claim for £30 for treating five soldiers and four soldiers' wives who were 'blown up on the march to the Battle of Culloden' – presumably this was an accidental explosion of gunpowder. Authority demurred at the amount, and the doctor in question was eventually paid £15 in 1753. There was a small detachment of troops in Berwick upon Tweed, and in 1762 a civilian doctor refused to treat them because his bill for the previous two years remained unpaid. He got his money eventually. What must strike the present-day reader as rather more than curious is that wounded men were treated in an extremely casual manner, and often left to fend for themselves. Three gunners each lost a limb at the Battle of Fontenoy in 1745, and apparently made their own way back to their depot at Woolwich. They had to petition for payment of their travelling expenses, and eventually were paid one guinea (£1.05) each – a settlement which the army regarded as generous.

The first authentic voice of a soldier in a military hosptial is that of Corporal Todd of the 30th Foot who, in 1757, was admitted to the hospital at Portsmouth with a sickness that he does not specify. He found that new admissions were assigned to wards 'according to our different disorders'. The diet he found meagre, consisting of broth, milk, rice and a pound of bread daily, but no meat. While he was in hospital his regiment moved to Berkshire. He was discharged, and had to make his own way there in easy stages. He went sick again while the regiment was in Reading, and here he was tended by a civilian doctor. Todd appreciated these ministrations, saying that if he and his fellow sufferers had been left to the care of the regimental surgeon he 'would have killed us'.

There were, of course, devoted and skilful doctors serving with the army in the eighteenth century. One of them, R. Hamilton, was born in 1739 and died in 1830 aged ninety-one. He wrote a book entitled *The Duties of a Regimental Surgeon Considered etc.* which was published in 1787, and it throws a fascinating light upon army life towards the end of the century, with many references to the American Revolution. The book opens with some general comments on the status of a medical officer and the hospital arrangements for the unit:

> Each regiment, regular as well as Militia, is allowed a surgeon as he is termed and a surgeon's mate. Their business is to attend to the disease of the men at all times when-ever it is judged necessary. For this service the surgeon is allowed four shillings [20p] a day; the mate three and six pence [approx. 17p].

In practice, taking various stoppages of pay into account, the weekly sum worked out for the surgeon at one guinea (£1.05) per week. Both medical officers were exempted from all regimental duties and, since they were officially regarded as 'an appendage to the corps', they ranked below the youngest ensign. The duties of the regimental surgeon were many. Apart from treating the men who reported to him as sick, and attending punishment parades, he also ran a hospital. This, at a period when there were few barracks, would have been a house taken over for this purpose by the regiment and for which the government allowed £30 a year – a sum which had to cover rent, stores and the hire of a nurse at six pence (2½p) per day.

There was often great difficulty in finding suitable nurses for the hospital. She had to be 'good careful and tender', and her duties were:

> To be with the patient almost constantly, to administer drink and medicines with care and punctuality . . . to pay attention to the calls of nature, the way he lies in bed, the state of his tongue . . . and if at the same time he has blisters open, or other sores, either accidental or made as an assistance to his recovery, to keep them well dressed and as easy to his feelings as possible . . . What in the army is stiled a nurse . . . is more properly the housekeeper, she cooks and caters for all the patients in the hospital, makes drinks, and prepares other medicines that require culinary treatment.

Nurses who did all this certainly earned their sixpence per day! Not unnaturally, because nurses were so poorly paid even by eighteenth-century standards, it was hard to recruit them, and in regiments where none could be found an 'orderly man' was detailed to tend the sick. This duty was apparently undertaken by a rota of men, each one doing twenty-

ABOVE & OPPOSITE: Soldiers invalided home from the Crimea in the Hospital Barracks, Brompton, 1855. They are all wearing hospital dress.

four hours in the hospital. Hamilton regarded this practice as quite unsatisfactory. 'What attention', he asks, 'can in general be expected from a clumsy, heedless soldier, ordered on a duty he greatly dislikes from its nature as well as the confinement to which it subjects him?'

Many soldiers would have been living in billets, usually public houses, where they were so little regarded by landlords and landladies that 'the places allotted to them are generally some uninhabited garret or lumber room where the very air they are obliged to breathe is so vitiated, as, at first entrance, considerably to affect a person unaccustomed to it.' Visiting men who were sick in quarters was a matter of some concern to Hamilton, who despaired of his patients. They were, he wrote, 'destitute frequently of everything . . . destitute of a proper bed to lie on . . . destitute of food or cordials . . . which are absolutely and indispensably necessary for recovery. The truth is that many a prisoner in his cell is better lodged than we find many of the soldiery in billets.' There is, Hamilton admits, something that can be said for publicans – they are 'greatly oppressed, especially in time of war, by the military'; and he suggests that soldiers might be better done by if they were billeted on butchers or bakers. The theme running through Hamilton's book is that of the adverse conditions in which sick men were, perforce, confined. He mentions, too, the problems that soldiers had in 'maintaining a decent standard of cleanliness'; and failure to achieve this would have contributed to sickness and the spread of infection. In one room measuring twelve feet by fifteen feet which Hamilton visited, a dozen soldiers, some with acute fevers and others whom he calls chronic cases, lay in beds with no space between them.

For casualties abroad, especially in the tropics, conditions for the sick and wounded can only be guessed at. Private Downing of the 20th Foot was wounded at the Battle of Alexandria in 1801, and eventually lost his sight. In a verse account of his soldiering days he described how agonising was the treatment he received in a military hospital in Egypt. Two lines ran: 'But what did more augment my pain/The place so swarmed with flies.' If conditions in military hospitals were bad, those in non-military ones would have been equally bad. In no other respect, perhaps, does the military experience mirror so accurately the civilian one as in medical science and treatment of the sick. As medical science advanced and as methods of treatment became more sophisticated, the lot of the soldier and his civilian counterpart in medical hands improved beyond all measure. In the meantime, between the years 1793 and 1815, a considerable force of British troops was destroyed in the West Indies by sickness and disease rather than by enemy action. These losses represented the highest casualties sustained by any British expeditionary force until the twentieth century. Service in the Caribbean had long been regarded as a death sentence by regiments posted to the area. In 1742, for example, nine deaths out of ten in Admiral Vernon's force were due to the ravages of illness rather than to French or Spanish muskets. Of the eighteen hundred men who took part in a rather peaceful campaign in Nicaragua from 1779 to 1780, fewer than four hundred survived, and most of the casualties occurred through ill health. The British force of 1793–1815 included

Scene in a military hospital, Portsea, 1855.

European mercenaries and black soldiers of the West India Regiments. They suffered 424,000 casualties, of which 75,000 were fatal; and the vast majority of the deaths were attributed to disease, with malaria and yellow fever rife. Because casualties amongst black troops were proportionately lower than amongst Europeans, one option facing the government was to increase the number of West India Regiments which were largely recruited from slaves born in the West Indies or in Africa. There were advantages in such a course of action: the black regiments were cheaper to maintain, and their soldiers were more suited to tropical service than white troops. The government in London, however, preferred to sacrifice white soldiers' lives rather than create a larger force of armed black soldiers. In coming to the decision not to expand the black regiments the government was no doubt greatly influenced by the powerful voice of West Indian trading interests, which had all along opposed the recruitment of black soldiers.

In an effort to improve the conditions that white troops endured, attempts were made to improve their diet. More fresh meat was issued, fresh vegetables and fruit were available; both the drinking of rum and its quality became increasingly subject to regulation; and, finally, it was proposed to modify uniforms to make them more suitable for wear in hot climates. All these attempts to increase the immunity of the men to sickness proved to be largely in vain. The trouble was that, in the eighteenth century, both the identification and the treatment of tropical diseases were for the most part ineffectual. No cure, for instance, existed for yellow fever. What was really needed for the defence of the Caribbean was an all-black garrison, inured to life in the tropics; but this the government would not countenance, and as a result a British army was destroyed by the ravages of tropical fever.

While this process of destruction was going on, the medical organisation of the army during the campaigns of 1793–1795 in the Low Countries broke down completely. Certain reforms were thus instituted, the most important of which were that in 1796 army surgeons were granted equivalent military rank to officers, admitted to regular pay, and supplied with instruments and drugs at public expense. These reforms provided the foundation upon which the army's medical service developed during the Napoleonic Wars.

A Yorkshireman from Mickleton-in-Teesdale, William Dent, qualified as a doctor in 1810 after two years' training, and in the same year joined the 4th Foot as a Hospital Mate, General Service. His mother had demurred at his joining the army, and he wrote to her justifying his choice of a military career: 'I think the Army an excellent school for a young man who has a desire to excel either in his profession or to become acquainted with the manners of the world.' His service took him to many places, including Gibraltar where in 1810 he was appointed Assistant Surgeon to the 9th Foot, ranking as a subaltern and paid nine shillings (45p) per day. Later he went to Spain and Portugal, North America and the West Indies, and here, in 1824, he was appointed Surgeon to the 21st Foot with the rank of captain and fourteen shillings (70p) per day. In the same year he was drowned at sea while on his way home to England on leave. The letters that he wrote to his family over a fifteen-year period cover military rather than medical matters, but they do indicate that promotion for an army doctor could be very slow. Despite such tardiness, the presence in the army of professionals like Dent would have meant that wounded men and the sick received far better care than they had ever done before, crude though their treatment might appear by modern standards.

Sergeant Daniel Nicol of the 92nd Regiment was wounded at the Battle of Talavera in 1809, and recalled being well treated by his regimental surgeon:

> Using my firelock as a crutch . . . I kept hopping along until I came to a large white house where many wounded men were waiting to be dressed. Here I found the surgeon, Dr Beattie, who came at once to me and dressed my leg and put a bandage on it. He then gave me a drink of water and told me I had got it at last. I, smiling, replied, 'Long run the fox, but he is sure to be caught at last.' This made many smile whose bones were sore enough.

Nicol was lucky – he was able to walk to the doctor. The fate of those who could not do this was often uncertain. After a battle wounded men might lie on the field for anything up to three days before they were taken to hospital. The Battle of Salamanca (1812) was fought partly over ground which was overgrown with shrubs and had ravines which were full of nearly-ripe corn. Both these factors presented problems to the parties of men from various regiments who had been detailed to bring in their own wounded. A commissary officer noticed a group of about two hundred men on the slope of a hillock, to which they had either crept or been carried to await removal to hospital. Each man was wrapped in a blanket to distinguish him from the dead. This represents a grim prefiguring of the situation on the Western Front just over a century later. After engagements, wounded men lay in no man's land between opposing lines of trenches, often taking refuge in shell holes or lying in the mud, to be rescued, if they were lucky, by their comrades – sometimes at very considerable risk.

129

The hospital at Scutari in 1855 possessed a newly developed machine in which, it was claimed, 1000 articles of newly washed linen could be thoroughly dried in twenty-five minutes. The waste heat produced was used to heat a 100-gallon boiler; a washing trough and wringer were attached.

In the Peninsula, where the Duke of Wellington and his army fought the French, the journey to hospital for those men whose injuries prevented them from walking was agonising. Sitting or lying in rudely constructed, bullock-drawn Portuguese carts, with solid wheels revolving on unoiled axle-trees, the men would have suffered greatly as they proceeded at about two miles an hour on rough roads and stony tracks. Joseph Donaldson, a sergeant serving with the 94th Scots Brigade, described the vehicles:

> They were about five feet long, and two and a half broad; but, instead of being boarded at the sides, there were stakes placed in holes about eighteen inches apart; the wheels were about two feet in diameter, rather octagonal than round; and, as they were not girt with iron, it was quite a common thing to have a piece broken out of the circumference, and, of course, every time the wheel turned, the whole cart would be violently shook.

Sometimes wounded men might be conveyed on the backs of mules, or occasionally in English spring waggons which were marginally less uncomfortable. Once in hospital, the kind of treatment that a wounded man received might vary considerably. Almost always facilities were inadequate and services overstretched, particularly after a battle. In 1810 Sergeant J.S. Cooper of the 7th Foot was transported in the rain, in a jolting cart, to a hospital at Villa Viciosa. His arrival there was not auspicious:

> Not being able to walk without support, I remained on the cart till nearly night, and was then helped up the steps of a convent. The sick not being then disposed of, I was laid down on cold flags at the stair head, and left there till removed by order of the surgeon . . . I was

afterwards carried into a corridor among perhaps two hundred sick and dying men.

Here he lay in considerable discomfort, receiving no treatment and scant attention:

> One day a woman belonging to our regiment passed by my bed. I called her and asked her to bring me a little tea. I had several small loaves that I could not eat, under my pillow. These I gave her, but she forgot to bring the tea, though she often went by my couch of dried fern.

A few days later Cooper was sent to another hospital at Elvas, some sixteen miles away. He was conveyed there, with other casualties, in small covered waggons drawn by mules, a journey which he found more satisfactory than the earlier one. Conditions in the hospital were grim: twenty sick men in an unventilated room with one door. 'A little sympathy would have soothed, but sympathy there was none. The orderlies [men who acted as nurses to the sick] were brutes.' He survived because a doctor acceded to his request for more to eat and drink, and eventually rejoined his regiment.

Corporal W. Wheeler of the 51st Foot was more fortunate. Wounded in the leg, he was admitted to the General Hospital at Fontarabia in 1814. Here his wound turned septic, and he was moved to the incurable ward. Amputation of the limb was decided upon, but a Spanish doctor intervened and applied what Wheeler described as 'something like pepper and salt mixed' to his wound, bandaged it up, and in a few days the infection had cleared. One of the nurses, wife of a soldier, accidentally pricked her finger with an infected pin in the incurable ward, and died soon after. The poison in the wound – Wheeler refers to it as 'sluff' – was almost always lethal; he had been very lucky, and he knew it.

When the Napoleonic Wars ended with the defeat of the French at Waterloo in 1815, medals were for the first time awarded to officers and men alike – but little thought was given to the care of sick and wounded. When the Crimean War broke out in 1854, the lessons of the past from which something might have been learned had been forgotten. The incompetence which characterised the handling of the army throughout

Transport – whatever had to be carried – was always difficult in the Crimea where the terrain was often rough. These improvised ambulances are conveying wounded men in what look like armchairs mounted in pairs on mules.

131

the conflict with Russia make it apparent that military thinking about the conduct of a major war was non-existent. Since 1815 the army had become the bastion of an aristocracy which resisted any kind of change, and attempted to maintain a code of outmoded privileges in the face of far-reaching changes in society at large. The result was that the expeditionary force sent to the shores of the Black Sea suffered from shortages of food and equipment. Muddle and lack of organisation was nowhere more apparent than in the brutal and careless treatment of sick and wounded men in a field army fighting far from home. The story of Florence Nightingale's intervention into this tragic state of affairs, and her attempts to bring succour to the casualties of the Crimean War, is too well known to be retold here. It was this war which gave impetus to further improvements in the organisation of army medical services. Not until 1873, though, was the military doctor removed from regimental organisation and an Army Medical Staff, to which they all belonged, was formed. Eleven years later, in 1884, the Medical Staff Corps, consisting of officers and other ranks, was created; and in 1898 its title was changed to the Royal Army Medical Corps. Its nursing counterpart in the modern army, Queen Alexandra's Royal Army Nursing Corps, derives from the establishment in 1881 of the Army Nursing Service, which gave army nurses a corporate identity for the first time.

While the post-Crimean changes in the organisation of medical services was proceeding, the army was facing and attempting to cope with a major health problem: venereal disease. In 1859 a reluctant government had been prodded into setting up an Army Sanitary Commission which quickly made the discovery that soldiers stationed at home lived in such a filthy environment that their mortality rate was twice that of their civilian counterparts; and worse, in that year, out of every one thousand men admitted to hospital, four hundred and twenty-two of them were suffering from venereal disease. Even the most cautious of reformers was stirred by this figure, but the problem had to be approached very gingerly. Not only was the disease highly contagious, but there were all kinds of medical, legal and moral aspects. There was the feeling, too, that it was sapping the numerical strength of the army which was regarded as a very costly institution paid for with public money. Some attempt was being made to deal with the problem in India, as we have seen, but at home things were different. Both *The Times* and *The Lancet* urged reform: in this area of sanitation some kind of control by the military authorities was needed. In the correspondence columns of *The Times* an army chaplain lamented 'the sad specimens of depraved and degraded humanity' who plied their trade round army camps. Exhortation to a more virtuous life was recommended, and it was suggested that men should be lectured on the dangers of contagious diseases. Reading and recreation rooms were provided in newly-built barracks, but the problem remained acute because still the monotony and dreariness of garrison life drove men to what the *National Review* in 1863 called 'intemperance and debauchery'. What was required in this situation was legal control of prostitutes in garrison towns, but there was a marked reluctance to set any reforms in train, or

The newly-invented portable drying-closet donated by Angela Burdett-Coutts to the hospital at Scutari.

even in some quarters to discuss the matter at all. Florence Nightingale, an authority on disease in the army, might have been expected to speak up vigorously in favour of such control; but she preferred to pontificate about the causes of vice being physical and not moral, and urged that with proper environmental surroundings morality would take care of itself. Pressure for medical reform continued, and resulted eventually in an Act of Parliament in 1864 which gave the Army Medical Department extended powers to control venereal disease in towns frequented by troops. This was a start, and it did go some way to control the disease, although the number of infected men in 1867 remained high. The existence of a problem had at last been acknowledged, however, and the conditions under which soldiers lived began to improve. Equally important was the heightened public awareness of the need for a healthy army.

One man who served in the ranks at this time was a Scot, William Hamilton, who was born in 1840. When he was twenty he joined the Ross-shire Militia, and on its disbandment some months later he joined the 93rd Highlanders, transferring in 1863 to the Army Hospital Corps whose members were soldier hospital orderlies. His autobiography, published in several issues of the *Royal Army Medical Journal* during 1974 and 1975, provides an interesting view of other-rank life in the medical services in the later years of the nineteenth century, but is effect is somewhat marred by a prevailing tone of self-righteousness. He joined the Army Hospital Corps presumably because he found life as an infantry man dull – 'card playing and loafing about the canteen occupied the evenings of the ordinary soldier', he wrote. Prostitution is not mentioned at all in these pages, neither is there a mention of venereal disease, although it is inconceivable, surely, that he would not have come across soldiers suffering from contagious infections while he was working in army hospitals. As a Methodist and teetotaller, he does have something to say about drinking habits, and describes how different was the atmosphere in the Aldershot barracks he went to in 1872, when every regiment had a Temperance Society, from the one in which he had been stationed as an infantryman ten years earlier. The best parts of his autobiography are those which describe everyday happenings, like the situation he found when he was posted to Perth in 1867: 'The War Office and the Gas Company were at war over the price of gas, and candles and oil lamps were the only illuminations in the barracks and the hospital.'

More revealing, perhaps, of other-rank life in what has become the Royal Army Medical Corps are the memoirs of Edgar Wallace, who joined it in 1894. He had enlisted into the Royal West Kent Regiment when he was eighteen years old, and transferred to the Medical Staff Corps a year or two later:

> I had to go to hospital to have my tooth attended, and there I saw the comfortable quarters of the Medical Staff Corps. Nice beds, cosy sitting room and better pay. Also a private held some sort of position. His uniform was quietly blue with red facings; he wore a round cap and chin-strap of cavalry jauntiness. I gave the matter considerable thought . . .

Some time later Wallace paraded before his company commander and formally requested permission to transfer out of his regiment. Formal application was made and sent to the appropriate authority. One contemporary, an old soldier, was scathing in his comment: 'What do you want to go an' mix poultices for? And you a teetotaller! You'll be dead in a month!'

The training in the MSC at Aldershot Wallace described as 'heavy', mostly classes in anatomy and drill. Most of the sergeants and corporals who instructed him were also dispensers, and several were able to draw teeth. When he passed out as trained he was posted to No. 2 Hospital North Camp, where he was put in charge of a ward containing twenty-four soldiers, each suffering from syphilis. No woman nurse worked at what a sister at the Cambridge Hospital, Aldershot, referred to as 'the dirty hospital', and Wallace found the work interesting after he had got over his 'repugnance to handling the sheets and bed linen . . . had taken a few dead men to the mortuary and learned to dissect them for post-mortem purposes . . .' He was posted to South Africa in 1896, and sent to a small hospital with only four beds at Simons Town. There was a staff of four: surgeon, sergeant, orderly and cook. While he was stationed here Wallace began in journalism, and his success led to his applying for his discharge from the army. He was, his colonel told him, earning too much money and demoralising the detachment.

By the time the Boer War broke out in 1899, the Royal Army Medical Corps was prepared to operate in the field. Every battalion or equivalent unit had its own medical officer and a staff of two ambulance drivers, besides one corporal and one private. There was a medical section commanded by a major attached to each brigade; a field hospital was attached to every divison and was commanded by a lieutenant-colonel; there were lines of communication and base hospitals; and altogether the preparation for war was thorough and, for the most part, stood the test of active service well.

One of the most important innovations which made the life of a wounded soldier much more comfortable than it would otherwise have been was the hospital train. Robert Blatchford, who had served as a sergeant with the 103rd Foot, was discharged in 1877. At the end of the memoir he wrote of his military experience, *My Life in the Army* (1910), he includes a description of what must have been one of the earliest purpose-built hospital trains, written by his daughter Winifred who accompanied him on a visit to army exercises in the Vale of the White Horse some time before the outbreak of the Second Boer War in 1899:

> One night an officer kindly took us to see a carriage of the hospital-train. It was a beautiful thing – a long railway-coach, painted white, and spotlessly clean, hung with cots like bunks in a ship's cabin. The beds were made upon strong spring mattresses to evade vibration when the train is moving. These trains are run as near to the scene of action as possible, and are, of course, for the wounded. Each train has six coaches, and each coach holds twelve beds, and, I believe, four couches. Then to each coach there is a kitchen, an officers' compartment, and lockers for medicines, wines, foods, etc.

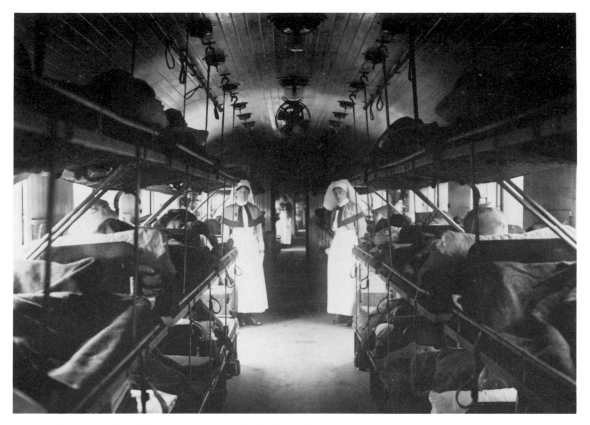

Hospital trains, often like the one described above but sometimes more makeshift, played an important role in South Africa and during the Great War, where casualty figures were higher than they had ever been before. Kingsley Martin, who was to become a distinguished journalist, served in France from mid-summer 1916 with the Friends Ambulance Unit, and was an orderly on a hospital train. In his autobiography, *Father Figures* published in 1966, he described some of his experiences:

A hospital train of the First World War.

> Two of us worked in the ward, a couple of doctors and two or three nurses lived in the central coaches. Each coach was arranged to take twenty lying patients, with floor-space on which to dump five or more stretchers if necessary. Alternatively, forty or fifty men could sit in the coach if they were walking cases. All the equipment had to be on the basis of self-sufficiency. There were two pails for soup or cocoa or tea, a brass urn for drinking water – if you were lucky enough to find it – and little candle lamps on brackets, which had to be continuously polished and which were kept bright by woollen caps which kindly ladies had made for the heads of soldiers. A primus stove was the most important object: a good deal of life turned on the question of whether one could get enough paraffin by fair means or foul.

He talks, too, of a load of dysentery cases taken to Le Havre and the problem of dealing with bedpans in the restricted space of a loaded railway coach. Another difficulty was that some of the rolling stock had no corridors running their length:

135

There was an excting side to being without corridors. The foot-boards were broad and adequately provided with hand-holds. That again was all right in the daytime, and if you were not carrying anything. But it was risky on a dark night and in bad weather. I think I rather enjoyed this; it was exhilarating. If you climbed out on the track side – perhaps you had to fetch a doctor for a too sick patient – you went out at some peril. You pushed the door against what felt like the solid opposition of rushing air, and then felt it seized from your hand and slammed back against the side of the train . . .

The wounded men, said Kingsley Martin, were incredibly patient and unhappy. He mentions the deep depression of wounded black soldiers and the large number of S.I.W. (self-inflicted wound) cases which occurred in the army during 1918; and he tells of his first experience of mustard gas casualties during the German push in March 1918. This moving and graphic account of life on a hospital train at this period is, I believe, unique.

During the Second World War hospital trains were widely used, and they are still to be found in today's army. It was, though, the Great War, with its appallingly high rate of casualties, which saw so immense an expansion in the need for medical services and facilities. One of the least known was the use of barges in France and Flanders, each one 'commanded' by a corporal of the Royal Engineers, to transport wounded men in back areas. An innovation which, according to Captain J.A. Hayward of the RAMC, 'revolutionised the surgery of the war and was the means of saving thousands of lives' was the Casualty Clearing Station. This was a small mobile hospital staffed by doctors, nurses and orderlies just behind the firing line. It had been discovered that fatal sepsis and gangrene of wounds could be avoided if effective operations could be carried out within thirty-six hours; and now these stations provided immediate facilities for surgery, as well as being a crucial link between the battlefield and hospitals at the Base. Captain Hayward describes the strain and fatigue he experienced while operating upon one wounded man after another, over a thirty-six-hour period, and he mentions one orderly: 'A boy of twenty, he had served without relief for months . . . attending to the worst cases and the dying. He had all the patience, tenderness, and devotion of a woman, the gentle hands and skill of a nurse, and an enduring fortitude.'

The experience of the Great War, so painfully acquired, was neither lost nor forgotten. In the Second World War, and in the conflicts which followed it right up to the Falkland Island expedition and the continuing violence in Northern Ireland, the Royal Army Medical Corps has provided the highest standards of treatment available for wounded soldiers. Aeroplanes and helicopters are now used for the speedy evacuation of casualties – a practice far removed from the past when, after a battle, parties of soldiers and even camp followers would scour the field for wounded men.

Stretcher-bearers on the Western Front during the Battle of Thiepval, September 1916. The role of the men who collected the wounded and carried them to regimental aid posts, ambulance, or casualty clearing stations, was often difficult and dangerous. In the Ypres Salient, where the battle for Passchendaele was fought during autumn 1917, continual heavy rain turned the ground into a quagmire. Years later, a Canadian veteran recalled that it took six men to handle a stretcher in the mud.

Chapter 8

AFTER THE ARMY

There was a song in the army during the Great War, with words set irreverently to the tune of the hymn 'We are but little children weak', which went like this:

> We are but little soldiers weak,
> We only get six bob a week;
> The more we work, the more we may,
> It makes no difference to our pay.
>
> Oh, sergeant-major, I can't shoot,
> So give me back my civvy suit;
> And when this f — g war is over,
> Take me back to dear old Dover.

Another, sung in both world wars, was set equally irreverently to the tune of a well-known hymn, 'What a friend we have in Jesus'. It featured impressively in Joan Littlewood's show *Oh What a Lovely War*, which had its first public performance on 19 March 1963. It went as follows:

> When this f — g war is over,
> Oh, how happy I shall be!
> I shall get my civvy clothes on,
> No more soldiering for me.
> No more church parades on Sunday,
> No more asking for a pass,
> I shall tell the Sergeant Major
> To stick his passes up his arse.

There were two further stanzas, but the sense is adequately conveyed by this one. The sentiments expressed in both songs might lead one to suspect that all soldiers were simply waiting for the time – even counting the days – when they could leave the army; but this was not so. The voice we hear in the two songs was that of the wartime soldiers for whom service was an unwelcome intrusion into life, and who wanted above all to return to what was called 'civvy street'. The time-serving regular soldier might in a fit of irritation say 'Roll on my pontoon' (i.e. 21 years' service), but it was, I think, rarely meant, and when the time came there was often a marked reluctance to go. Loyalties could be strong – loyalty to comrades-in-arms, to a regiment, to a tradition, and above all to a way of life that became so ingrained in many an old soldier that any alternative to it was unthinkable and almost unreal. After a long period of service, with the very real security that it offered, life as a civilian could look very bleak indeed. For many men the army had become their family, and leaving it was an emotional matter.

For wartime soldiers things were rather different, and at the end of hostilities most of them were glad enough to leave the army. If a man was in good health it was always possible to slip back into civilian life, and if

Veterans, 1801.

he were fortunate, to find some sort of employment. William Wey, who had served as a private soldier in Lord Hale's Regiment of Foot in the army of William III, settled happily back into civilian life as a blacksmith in Tolpuddle, Dorset, in 1701, and his experience was probably typical of many men who served in wartime right down to the present day.

For wounded or debilitated men, however, the prospect was that both they and their families would face lives of considerable hardship. The earliest provision for such men had been enshrined in the Statute for Maimed Soldiers of 1593, but this lapsed on the outbreak of the Civil War in 1642. In order to provide some help for men who were discharged from the army as unfit because of a wound or loss of limb, Parliament ordered in 1643 that collections of money should be made in every parish throughout the country for relief purposes. Any ex-soldier or his widow seeking help had to produce a certificate from the last commander under whom he had served and later, as a safeguard against fraud, a second certificate from the regimental surgeon had to be presented to the parish. This fund seems to have been known as the Lame Soldier Rate, and we can glimpse some of the problems its administrators faced, and how they tackled them, from the following records of the Michaelmas Sessions at Maidstone, Kent, in 1652 and 1653 respectively:

> It is ordered by this court that Mr Herbert, the Treasurer for the Maymed Souldiers, shall and doe forthwith pay and allowe unto Ann Whitehead, the relicte of John Whitehead, who lost his life in the Parliament's service, the somme of two shillings six pence weekly to commence from the day of the date hereof and to continue unto the first day of February next ensewing and the overseers of the poore of Gravesend in this countie are hereby ordered that they shall and doe sette the said Ann to worke whereby shee may gayne by her labour soe much as may make upp the said two shillings and sixe pence at the least foure shillings by the weeke according to the statute in the case made and provided.

The second judgement concerned a wounded man:

> It is ordered by this court that Mr Herbert, the Treasurer for the County Stocke of these westerne partes of Kent, shall and doe forthwith pay unto Roger Valentine, a souldier who lost the use of his limns at the Worcester fight, the somme of twentie shillings to and for his present releife. And it is further desired by this court that the Governours of St. Thomas Hospital in Southwarke will receive the said Roger Valentine and take such care of him for his care as they shall thinke fitt.

These cases must indicate the pattern of applications for financial aid throughout the country, and perhaps in some districts the burden was a considerable one.

At the Restoration, hospitals and pensions for wounded and needy soldiers came to an end. The 140 or so men who were still languishing in hospital beds were discharged, and about 1,500 widows and orphans who were by that date receiving tiny pensions from the government were thrown upon the mercy of parish authorities where they lived. It was up to justices of the peace and overseers of the poor to make what provision they saw fit for the casualties of war. In 1681 King Charles II initiated the establishment of the Royal Hospital, Chelsea, intended as a refuge for veterans of twenty years and more of military service. Those who sought admission had to present two certificates: one signed by the Commissary-General of the Musters and the other by the applicant's commanding officer. By 4 March 1690, 472 places in the hospital had been taken up, and there were 107 'out pensioners' who drew allowances from the Royal Hospital but lived in their own lodgings. Despite its best efforts the Chelsea Hospital could hardly cope with all those men discharged from the army who applied, and it was full to overflowing as soon as it opened. The enterprise was designed with the needs of a domestic army in mind, and nobody seems to have thought about what would happen if an augmented force, fighting abroad, should send home numerous casualties. Very soon attempts were made to weed out the elderly but still fit men from the sick and wounded, so that the former could be sent to join 'invalid companies' whose ranks were filled by 'out pensioners'. This had only a partial success, and the problems of elderly and maimed veterans of war were to haunt the army and the public at large for many years to come. Think, for example, of the limbless and blind ex-servicemen singing in the streets of towns and cities in Great Britain during the 1920s . . .

Men who left the army unwounded after a period of service at the turn of the seventeenth and eighteenth centuries received fourteen days' pay; they were entitled to keep certain items of equipment, and were given a three shilling (15p) bounty in exchange for their swords – except for sergeants who were expected to keep theirs. In the reign of Queen Anne, provision was roughly the same, the bayonet ranking with the sword for the extra three shillings. There was also a legal entitlement for an ex-soldier (provided that he was not a deserter) to practise a trade 'irrespective of the rules about apprenticeship, without any let, suit, or molestation of any person or persons whatsoever'. Craftsmen and skilled artisans amongst regular soldiers almost certainly made up a small minority, but they were given a degree of protection and help in the form of 'three years exemption from distrainment of person, tools, or stock for debt owing when he enlisted'.

Meagre provision for the ex-soldier continued into the twentieth century. Indeed, the very term 'ex-serviceman' still carries the overtones of need and indigence which it evoked when army pensions were very much more niggardly than they are today. However small, the pension was worth having; and it was not unknown for a man who had left the army after a period of satisfactory service to apply for a pension long after his discharge – when, perhaps, he was growing old and infirm. Sergeant Roger Lamb was such a one. Enlisting in 1773 when he was seventeen years old, he served for a number of years with the 9th and 23rd Regiments of Foot, most of this service in North America during the War of Independence. He quitted the army in 1784 and became a schoolmaster in Dublin; but in 1809, finding himself in straitened circumstances in retirement, he addressed a 'Memorial' to the Duke of York as Commander-in-Chief of the army, requesting an army pension. Some three weeks later he received a favourable reply: authority had been given 'for placing him upon the Out Pension of Chelsea Hospital, dispensing with his appearance before the Board.'

Lamb was perhaps fortunate, not least in the celerity with which his request was dealt with. Another old soldier had good fortune in another way. His death was reported in *The Essex Chronicle* of 10 August 1827:

> Lately, in White Horse-lane, Canterbury, at the advanced age of 105 years, a veteran soldier named Williams. He was a drum-boy at the Battle of Culloden, which battle terminated the hopes of the House of Stuart in this country. He was also present at the battle of Bunker's Hill near Boston, the first time the Americans attempted to resist the

OPPOSITE:
Two veterans, inmates of the Royal Hospital, Chelsea, watching a lance-corporal of the 25th Cyclists Battalion riding past, *c.* 1900.

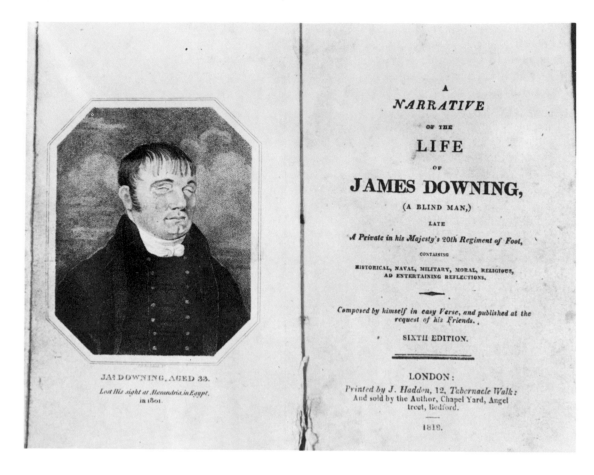

The title page and frontispiece of Private Downing's verse autobiography.

British troops in the field. The veteran had enjoyed a pension for the last 45 years.

Another veteran, ex-Sergeant Benjamin Miller who had served in the Royal Artillery from 1796 to 1815, drew his pension of one shilling six and a half pence (about 8p) per day until his death at the age of eighty-eight in 1865. He lived in the village of Melbury Osmond in Somerset, and used to hire a cart and drive with other old soldiers into Yeovil once a quarter to collect the money. In his diaries the Reverend Francis Kilvert described meeting 'The Old Soldier' (John Morgan) who lived at Bronith near Clyro. On 16 June 1870 he showed Kilvert his Peninsula medal with clasps for Vittoria, Pyrenees and Toulouse. In April 1871 Morgan was awarded a pension of nine pence (i.e. almost 4p) per day by the Chelsea Hospital, backdated to February of that year.

One of the most enterprising army pensioners that I have come across was Private James Downing, mentioned in the previous chapter, who lost his sight while serving with the 20th Foot at the Battle of Alexandra in 1801. He was a Bedford man, and from his house or lodging in Chapel Yard, Angel Street, issued a ninety-six-page autobiography written in verse. It ran to at least six editions, and as the author said in a Preface, his book 'in some little degree aided the limited pension allowed by the government'. Despite a depressingly moralistic tone, the work does contain some splendid little cameos of military life. There is, for example, the account of a sergeant on a troopship who came on deck for a breath of air on a warm night – and fell overboard:

As I was here one night on watch,
The moon shone very clear,
A sergeant came upon the deck,
To breathe a purer air.

Who could have thought his time so short,
He scarce refreshment found,
Before he fell into the sea,
And instantly was drown'd!

Perhaps it is worth making the point that credible ex-soldiers rarely turn up in fiction. Amongst those who do, and are in some way memorable, is Corporal Brewster, veteran of the Battle of Waterloo and central character in a short story by Sir Arthur Conan Doyle entitled 'A Straggler of '15'. The narrative itself has as its background the Woolwich garrison, and the corporal is drawn with rare fidelity. Then there is ex-Sergeant Bunter, who served with Lord Peter Wimsey on the Western Front. A man of considerable resource, he featured in several novels and short stories by Dorothy L. Sayers. In Charles Dickens' novel *Bleak House* there are two old soldiers, George Rouncewell and Matthew Bagnet. Both are skilfully drawn: Rouncewell embodies many military virtues, as befits an ex-cavalryman, while Bagnet, an ex-artilleryman, is one of the most finely drawn minor characters in the novel. His wife is one of the few other rank army wives to appear in fiction, and his children were known as Woolwich, Quebec and Malta, denoting the places where their father was stationed when they were born. It is not clear whether Rouncewell and Bagnet were pensioners, but both ran successful businesses and the probability is that there were in the nineteenth century some old soldiers just like them. It is also interesting that both men are more lovingly chronicled by Dickens than the rather unpleasant ex-officer Major Bagstock in *Dombey and Son*.

Fiction apart, Henry Mayhew tells us that he came across three kinds of ex-soldier on the streets in Victorian times. First there was the genuine veteran, reduced after service to mendicancy. 'Ragged though he be, there is a certain smartness about the soldier proper, observable in the polish of his boots, the cock of his cap, and the disposition of the leather strap under his lower lip.' He is always, says Mayhew, ready to work for his living and hates begging. Then there is the man who has been discharged dishonourably, 'the most dangerous and violent of mendicants', who preys upon society when he can. Finally there is the imposter who puts on an old military coat and claims to have fought in the Crimean War or to have taken part in the Indian Mutiny.

The number of regular soldiers leaving the army on pension or otherwise has formed a steady trickle over the years. From 1885, men were assisted by the National Association for the Employment of Ex-soldiers; by 1914 it had become the largest employment-finding agency in Britain, with not less than 110 branches. Even the great periods of demobilisation and disbandments of regiments which followed the Civil War, the Napoleonic War, to say nothing of lesser wars over the centuries, have scarcely represented a flood of men resettling into civilian life, and although there were attendant difficulties and dislocations, these were as nothing when compared with the problems of demobilising the armies which had been built up to fight the Great War and the Second World War.

Despite an elaborate scheme drawn up by the Ministry of Reconstruction to provide orderly demobilisation and to avoid mass unemployment, 1918 found the authorities ill-prepared. When the armistice was signed there were about 3,750,000 men serving in the army, a figure which must be compared with 247,432 men who had made up its effective strength in August 1914. The task facing the government was, on the one hand, to preserve a much smaller, balanced regular force based on voluntary enlistment, and on the other to release from service in the fairest and most expeditious manner all those who wished to leave. It cannot be said that they succeeded in either objective. The initial post-war army – by 1922 it consisted of less than 220,000 men – was young and only partially trained. Too many experienced men, many of them senior NCOs and warrant officers, a proportion of them specialists of one kind or another, left the army as soon as they could. The speed of demobilisation was considerable: by November 1919 the effective strength of the army was under a million – although, oddly perhaps, recruiting figures were high.

Although the rundown in numbers went ahead at a remarkable rate, many men stationed at home and abroad felt strongly about what they perceived to be the inequalities of a demobilisation scheme which released personnel with fairly short periods of service, while retaining some who had served for much longer. What reasons there may have been for this practice seem rarely to have been explained to the men concerned, until there was resort to public protest of a kind never before seen in the army. Early in 1919 some 10,000 men held a demonstration in Folkstone over the slowness of demobilisation, and there was similar unrest at the British base in Calais. At Osterley Park, to the west of London, some 150 soldiers seized their lorries and drove to Whitehall as a protest. Action of this kind all over the country was reported at the time in the local press, but in a rather sparse manner because military censorship, despite a general uncertainty about its powers, was still in force. Added to discontent over demobilisation, other grievances surfaced: there was too much 'red-tape', including compulsory church parades; food was often bad; conditions in some camps – with reveille at 5.30 a.m. – were poor. Inevitably after the war there was a reduced willingness on the part of many men to accept without question the restrictions that the army placed on them. Finally, there was the question of providing a force to fight the Bolsheviks in Archangel and Murmansk. There seems to have been great resistance to this amongst serving soldiers, for a variety of reasons, and in March 1919 Lieutenant Colonel Radcliffe reported to the Deputy Chief of the Imperial General Staff on 'the unreliable state of the troops' serving in Russia under Generals Maynard and Ironside.

Times were unusual, and the War Office dealt with most of the discontent and unrest in a more sympathetic way than one might have expected. This was largely because authority had little room for manoeuvre. Large numbers of soldiers, supported by much of the press, were intent upon immediate honourable discharge. They considered, not without good justification, that they had done their duty, and they just wanted to go home. In this climate, with the memory of the Russian Revolution fresh in people's minds, wise counsels prevailed. Too heavy a hand in dealing with what were undoubtedly acts of insubordination and breaches of military discipline would almost certainly have adversely affected recruiting figures and damaged the army's reputation. In all probability, too, there would have been social unrest and riots in the streets, prompting the unthinkable question about whether, in the event of such happenings, the army could be relied upon to maintain order.

So problems were largely settled: the men went home and passions cooled. Indeed, when the mood of post-war euphoria had passed, some experienced ex-NCOs and men rejoined the army; and some regular soldiers who had been granted commissions during the war and, as officers, had become 'temporary gentlemen', reappeared in other units, often as warrant officers – or as sergeants. Few voices have come down to us from these turbulent days which followed the end of the war. One of them, that of Sapper Fred Thomas of the Royal Engineers, was muted, but extremely effective in the laconic way that it hinted at rising tension over this issue of demobilisation. Thomas served with the Egyptian Expeditionary Force from 1917 to 1920, and kept a diary which was beautifully reprinted with photographs by Pryor Publications in 1985 as *Uncle Fred's War*. On 15 November, only four days after the armistice had become effective, GHQ in Egypt was telling officers and NCOs to be tactful in dealing with their men, and ordered 'Give them sports and make duties as light as possible.' Ten days later there was lecture on demobilisation and many questions were asked. 'The terms', said Thomas, 'are likely to cause trouble.' At another lecture two days later an 'awkward' question put by a corporal went unanswered. Then, just before Christmas 1918, the Egyptian Labour Corps was sent home and its tasks, which included road repairing and unloading ships, were taken over by the 75th Division who had been on active service thoughout the war. Many of the men refused to do the work, and the intervention of General Lloyd, the local commander, proved fruitless, so the men were sent back to camp. Sapper Thomas was full of foreboding, and sensed trouble brewing everywhere. He commented, too, that the officers were enjoying themselves while the men were hard at work in North African sun. Demobilisation proceeded gradually, and Thomas himself went home in January 1920, his discharge coming in the following month.

Matters were handled much more intelligently after the Second World War. Soldiers of both sexes were allotted a release number based on age and length of service. Brightly printed notices giving precise details were posted in all camps, and there was a choice of several release dates for each number. A man or woman who enlisted, for example, in April 1942 at the

Cover of what was probably a popular early Victorian song. Since the latest engagement recorded upon it is Sobraon, which was fought in India in 1846, it almost certainly dates from before the outbreak of the Crimean War in 1854.

age of eighteen had a release number of 46, which meant that he or she would leave the army on any one of several dates between the end of December 1946 and the first half of January 1947. Once the army administration had been effected, and soldiers had been brought back from overseas, they would be issued with a suit of civilian clothes from a 'demob centre' and then go on a period of 'release leave' during which full pay and allowances were drawn. A small lump-sum bounty was also paid. The use of a sensible system which was seen to be fair meant that the disturbances which had accompanied demobilisation at the end of the Great War were largely avoided in the second one. There was admittedly some trouble in a few camps in the Far East, but it was dealt with immediately and some men prominent in it were courtmartialled, and for the most part the rundown of the army was extremely effectively accomplished.

There were other factors in this largely trouble-free demobilisation process in the late 1940s. One was the sheer quantity of well-presented information regarding jobs, career prospects and entry to higher education which was readily available to all men and women about to leave the service. Another was the Army Education Scheme 'Release Period' 1945–1948, under which instruction was given in a wide range of subjects and skills, often by men and women drawn from the ranks of the army and sometimes by civilians. The army also set up a number of residential institutions where all ranks of both sexes could undergo a four-week residential course in a wide range of academic subjects. They were called Formation Colleges, and while some of them were located in military camps, others were in beautiful premises like Newbattle Abbey near Edinburgh, Luton Hoo, Welbeck Abbey, the University of Göttingen (part of which became CORA – College of the Rhine Army), Mount Carmel and Perugia. These establishments were the nearest the army has ever come to providing, if not quite higher education, then certainly something covering more than the utilitarian subjects which had necessarily formed the curriculum of study for Army Certificates of Education. Staffed by soldiers – some of whom went on to achieve academic prominence – the Formation Colleges were a resounding success, and are recalled today, I suspect, with a very special pleasure by many who attended them. The successful running of the education scheme was due in large measure to the work of personnel serving in the Royal Army Educational Corps, which expanded its numbers at the end of the war. Today it is an all-officer corps, but then many of its members were non-commissioned and warrant officers. Applications to transfer to the corps were circulated throughout the army. Promising applicants were interviewed and, if deemed suitable, sent off after an interval of some weeks to Cuerden Hall, Bamber Bridge, near Preston in Lancashire, where two-week transfer courses were held. Each successful candidate was transferred to the RAEC as a sergeant instructor and posted to a unit where he or she might take over the running of an education scheme or be one of the staff in an education centre. Clearly there was an element of urgency which underlay the whole process, but the army was able to tap a wide range of talent and intelligence in its ranks in a way that had never been attempted before.

Today things are rather different for regulars leaving the army. The numbers involved are not large, and it is possible to ensure that every soldier who wishes to do so can undergo some sort of resettlement course or training, and also receive counselling as to possibilities and opportunities in civilian life. Certainly no honourably discharged soldier today need leave without some kind of preparation for life outside the army. For men and women who leave after a short period of service the problem is not a difficult one; but for those who have served for many years the break can seem severe. Of course there is a pension or a gratuity, but emotional links with the army are often very strong. Membership of a regimental association, and receipt of a regimental journal which keeps old soldiers in touch with news, can help to make things more bearable.

Despite all these provisions it is something of a shock to realise that, unlike many employers in the private sector, the army does not grant automatic death-in-service compensation for its personnel. What this means in practice is that the families and dependants of soldiers who are killed may have a very difficult time financially unless the soldier has contributed to a superannuation scheme. If he has done this, then his widow will receive a pension based upon his age, rank and length of service. Another option for a soldier is to join the Army Dependants Association (a sort of unit trust scheme), and in that case, in the event of his death, dependants would receive a monthly sum related to the number of units purchased until the date when he would have been fifty-five. Young unmarried soldiers are said to be unlikely to make this kind of provision, so there is another scheme for buying life cover through membership of the Single Soldiers Dependants Fund, which would entitle a person nominated by the soldier to a lump sum on his death and a once-a-year payment. The DHSS pays a widow's pension plus allowances for dependant children, and has in fact a more liberal policy with regard to 'common law' wives and pregnant girl friends than the army. Indeed, the army does not recognise such dependants and never has done so. Each case of this kind would be considered on its merits. If a soldier with dependant relatives were to be killed in Northern Ireland, the relatives could then make out a case for the Criminal Injuries Board in that province to consider.

The army, it is true, offers an excellent financial advice service to all ranks, but there is no doubt that unless a soldier makes individual provision, at his own cost, for the future of his dependants in case he is killed, those he leaves behind are likely to suffer considerable hardship. This is particularly true if the family occupies army quarters to which they have no right once his service ends. The main army charity, Soldiers' Sailors' and Airmen's Families Association (SSAFA), is always approachable and ready to help, and so too are various regimental associations, but such assistance cannot in the nature of things offer more than passing succour in time of pressing need and emotional distress.

The fact that army families may have to turn to charity at a time of great crisis verges upon what one newspaper in April 1988 described as 'the scandal of army compensation'. What is required is a comprehensive scheme, at no cost to individual soldiers, which will take care of bereaved families no less than personnel who are disabled. There should be no question of dependants having to 'make a case' for cash payments to an anonymous board, however well intentioned its members may be. That we do not yet have such a scheme – nor, it must be said, does there seem any likelihood of it – underlines the traditional niggardliness and insensitivity of governmental attitudes to the army – an army of which so much is expected, and of whose achievements those in power are so happy to boast.

AFTERWORD

For most regular soldiers the regiment or corps into which they enlisted and subsequently served their time remained the focus of individual loyalty. At its best a soldier's unit could represent his home, even his family, and all aspects of its daily round and ritual lay at the heart of British military life. It would be difficult to overestimate the great part which regimental tradition has played in the history of the army – although whether this is still so true of the late twentieth century is not entirely certain. Many of the older regiments have disappeared with the amalgamations between 1958 and 1970, and their places have been taken by units with new titles. The Queen's Regiment, for example, was formed on 31 December 1966 by the amalgamation of four infantry regiments which were themselves the result of previous amalgamations dating from 1959. Today, therefore, it can trace its ancestry back to no less then ten regiments of foot which existed in 1880 when the army deployed thirty-one cavalry regiments with various titles and 109 of infantry, most of these identified by their numbers. In 1881 the foot regiments were reorganised on the basis of county formations. Thus, to take one example, the Essex Regiment (now incorporated into the Royal Anglians) was formed by the amalgamation of the 44th and 56th Foot which became , respectively, the 1st and 2nd Battalions.

There are regiments which have never been subject to amalgamation, and these include the Green Howards, the Cheshire Regiment, the Royal Welch Fusiliers, the King's Own Scottish Borderers. The oldest infantry regiment is the Royal Scots (1st Foot), which was formed in 1633 when King Charles I issued a Warrant authorising Colonel Sir John Hepburn to raise a Scottish regiment for the French service. It became part of the British army in 1661, and its nickname 'Pontius Pilate's Bodyguard' is said to date from the early years of the regiment when its seniority was disputed by officers of a French unit with which it was serving.

Traditions, then, are less easy to maintain today, but in the past the army has sometimes clung to old ways and been resistant to change. An example of this is to be found in the way that regulations concerning the nomenclature of individual regiments were observed. When the standing army – precursor of the modern regular army – was formed by King Charles II, a regiment was known by the name of the colonel who commanded it and had, in many cases, raised it – there were Lillingston's, Peyton's, and so on. This practice had been established by both sides during the English Civil War, but by the end of the seventeenth century it was increasingly felt to be distressingly ephemeral because when there was a change of commanding officer – and this might happen frequently – the title of the regiment had to change. A Royal Warrant of 1694 authorised the numbering of regiments according to their seniority or the date when

149

they were raised; but little notice seems to have been taken of this authorisation, and in 1743 another Warrant ordered that the number of each regiment should be emblazoned on its colours. The King's army which fought at the battle of Culloden in 1746 were still more readily identified by their colonels' names than their numbers: there were Howard's, Barrell's, Wolfe's, Pultney's and the like. Yet another Warrant in 1751 laid it down that regiments would be identified by their numbers, but during the Seven Years War (1756–1763) many units continued to be referred to by their colonels' names. For many serving soldiers it was a matter of custom to talk of 'Brudenell's' rather than the 51st Foot.

The 1751 Warrant also decreed that regiments might, in addition to their numbers, be known by certain titular distinctions which were in common use. The 3rd Foot provides a case in point. From 1738 to 1749 it was commanded by Colonel Thomas Howard. In order to distinguish the regiment from another commanded by an officer with the same name, and because its scarlet jackets had buff facings, it became known as the Buff Howards, and eventually simply as The Buffs. By this name the regiment was readily identified until 1961, 210 years after it had been officially designated the 3rd (or The Buffs) Regiment of Foot. Today it is one of the ten regiments mentioned earlier who make up the Queen's Regiment. The change in 1881 to a 'county regiment' nomenclature for most infantry units was not entirely without precedent, for about a century earlier, in 1782, certain infantry formations were permitted to adopt territorial or county sub-titles. The 19th Foot became the 19th (1st Yorkshire North Riding) Regiment of Foot; and after several name changes it became, in 1921, the Green Howards, by which title it is still known. It is, as we have seen, one of the few infantry regiments to escape amalgamation.

For those devoted to the old ways the story of regimental amalgamation, and even disbandment, must make melancholy reading, inevitable though it has been. During the inter-war years the mechanisation of cavalry regiments was proceeding quickly, so that when the Royal Armoured Corps was formed in April 1939 many of its constituent units with titles like 4th/7th Royal Dragoon Guards, 14th/20th King's Hussars, 17th/21st Lancers, were the products of amalgamations which had taken place in the 1920s. For infantry regiments – with the exception of the Irish ones, which were disbanded in 1922 when the Irish Free State was established – the great period of change came mostly in the 1960s and 1970s. Two regiments refused to be amalgamated: the Cameronians and the York and Lancaster Regiment. They were simply disbanded; their traditions live on only in the memories of ex-soldiers and in the regimental museums at Hamilton in Lanarkshire and Sheffield respectively. Disbandment must seem a very drastic way of preserving regimental identity, and while no others went so far as the two mentioned, feelings about merging or disbanding often ran high. This was the case with the Argyll and Sutherland Highlanders, who were threatened with disbandment in 1970. It was a regiment with a proud tradition. They had been (as the 93rd Foot) the original 'Thin Red Line' at the battle of Balaclava in 1854, and during the relief of Lucknow in 1857 they had gained six Victoria Crosses.

OPPOSITE:
A recruiting poster of the 1920s, showing the extent to which the county regiments depended on and reflected local pride.

151

GONE FOR A SOLDIER

Twenty-seven battalions served with distinction during the Great War, and their record was equally gallant in the Second World War. Public outcry was immediate, and so insistent that the regiment was allowed to survive as a single company aptly named the 'Balaclava Company'; and two years later it was re-formed into a regular battalion. It is likely that without the campaign waged by the tabloid press and its exploitation of an unusually charismatic commanding officer, this Highland regiment, despite its tradition and unique identity, would not have survived.

For the soldier serving in the ranks, regimental identity expressed itself in various ways. When scarlet coats were worn, different coloured facings distinguished individual regiments. Cavalry regiments had especially elaborate uniforms, recalled sometimes in nicknames – the 11th Hussars wore crimson overalls in 1841 and were known as the Cherry Bums. Badges of non-commissioned and warrant rank would vary between regiments, and such differences are held to enhance both *esprit de corps* and loyalty to one's regiment. Similarly badges of individual units were, and still are, an important factor in fostering the sense of belonging. Field Marshal Montgomery realised this importance when he led the 8th Army in the Western Desert, and he became well known for wearing two badges in his beret. One denoted his senior rank: the other was that of the Royal Tank Regiment. It was an imaginative gesture and reflected the strong feelings that many soldiers had about the regiment or corps to which they belonged.

Two regiments have unusual practices with regard to cap badges. The Black Watch have since 1822 enjoyed the unique distinction of wearing a red hackle in their bonnets and no badge at all. The Gloucestershire Regiment has two cap badges, one at the back of the headdress as well as one at the front, this custom commemorating the action of the 28th Foot at the Battle of Alexandria in 1801 when they were attacked in the front and rear. The wearing of a back badge was officially confirmed in 1830, and 'back badge day' is still celebrated each year.

Regimental individuality comes in other forms. All ranks of the Royal Welch Fusiliers wear a black 'flash' or knot of black ribbons at the back of the collar. As the 23rd Foot this regiment was the last in the army to wear hair in pigtails or 'queues', and the 'flash' symbolises the black leather bag which was once used to sheath the pigtail and prevent its grease from soiling the soldier's jacket. Use of the black flash was officially sanctioned by King William IV in 1834. Its use could make a soldier very conspicuous. At a drill parade in Derby in 1943 Regimental Sergeant Major Gurney, MM, was drilling a squad of junior non-commissioned officers from several different infantry regiments. One of them was slightly out of position and the R.S.M., not knowing him by name, roared: 'That fusilier fellow! Pick up your dressing!' We all knew who was being addressed in this summary fashion and kept very still, while Corporal Welby, Royal Welch Fusiliers, shuffled into the correct position . . . Sometimes the cloth badges worn on the sleeve just below the shoulder, which designated the division to which a soldier and his unit belonged (in ascending order army organisation went: battalion, brigade, division), might give an added

152

sense of cachet or pride. A whole range of imaginatively designed divisional badges were used in the Great War. During the Second they were also widely used, and one in particular was recognised even outside the army – the jerboa which designated the 7th Armoured Division. Their fighting qualities in North Africa earned them the soubriquet 'Desert Rats' – an appellation which was sometimes, incorrectly, applied to all the Allied troops who fought in the Desert.

Division was about as high as personal loyalty would go. It was unusual for soldiers to feel much attachment to large formations whose officers were faceless – they would regard themselves primarily as 'Worcesters', 'Lancashire Fusiliers', 'Gunners' or 'Sappers'. It is indeed a tribute to the leadership of Montgomery in the Desert that for a brief period his men probably did feel themselves to be part of a rather special army whose commander was known to them.

The wearing of uniform and regimental badges, distinctions of rank and decorations both for gallantry and for service, have been vital in establishing a sense of allegiance in the army. In the interest of tidiness and cheapness uniforms tended to become simpler towards the end of the eighteenth century, lace distinctions and facing colours giving way to greater standardisation. The adoption of the shako – a hat with a peak – in 1801 provided the opportunity for the general wearing of regimental badges. Distinctions of rank for non-commissioned and warrant officers, although to a great extent standardised, still show some interesting variations. It was the East India Company which pioneered the granting of medals to officers and men employed in military operations in India, and it was not until 1815 that the Prince Regent, following its example, suggested the bestowal of a silver medal on all personnel who had been present at the Battle of Waterloo or the engagements of the two preceding days. After this the granting of campaign and gallantry medals became customary.

Not unconnected with all these factors was, and still is, the sense of tradition which is so enhanced by the great occasions of public military ritual at which the British excel: trooping the colour, changing the guard at Buckingham Palace and the Tower of London, massed bands marching and counter-marching, and of course the Remembrance Day ceremonies held annually to commemorate the dead of two world wars. Less public rituals observed by individual regiments are also important. Back-badge Day celebrated by the Gloucesters on 21 March has been mentioned; and there is Cambrai Day (20 November) on which the Royal Tank Regiment recalled the attack by 378 massed tanks which smashed through the German line at Cambrai in 1917. In the past, regiments returning from long periods of service abroad would hold a ceremonial parade in their county town, and the regimental colours – always a powerfully emotive symbol in army ritual – would be laid up in the parish church. Until 1881 such regimental colours were carried into action, and often bore the marks of this. Such ceremonies and parades would always be accompanied by music from the regimental band, usually led by the bandmaster who would be a Warrant Officer ranking next in seniority to the Regimen-

Two badges of the 17th (Leicestershire) Regiment of Foot (from 1881, The Leicestershire Regiment). The top one is *c.* 1800, the lower is twentieth-century, pre-1946, after which it became The Royal Leicestershire Regiment, which was in turn incorporated in The Royal Anglian Regiment in 1964.

153

tal Sergeant Major. The British army has long been renowned for the quality of its music.

Traditions are mostly made from success in battle, but this is not always the case. In 1881 the 49th and 66th Foot became the Royal Berkshire Regiment, with headquarters in Reading. A year earlier the 66th had been on active service in Afghanistan, where they were overwhelmed by the enemy at the Battle of Maiwand. Because it was a defeat the name of the action could not be recorded as a battle honour, but the people of Berkshire raised a public subscription to erect a monument to the regiment which can still be seen in Forbury Gardens, Reading. One survivor of the battle was 'Bobbie', a pet dog who belonged to a sergeant who had been killed. Bobbie was brought home, Queen Victoria granted an audience, and he was presented with the Afghan Medal. Sadly he was run over in the following year, but his body was stuffed and still sits, wearing the campaign medal, in the Regimental Museum of the Royal Berkshire Regiment, now at Salisbury.

For many corps in the army formed to provide support for the fighting men – Medical, Ordnance, Transport and so on – the task of forging a tradition has been more difficult, particularly because they are very much younger in terms of their foundation than infantry regiments. The Royal Artillery and the Royal Engineers, both of which date effectively from 1716, have long and honourable traditions; and because of their prominence and achievement in battle, the Parachute Regiment, created less

This regimental band in the courtyard of St James's Palace in the late eighteenth century included a group of adult soldiers playing taxing instruments such as the serpent, together with a number of boys playing pipes and drums. Between the two groups are three Black soldiers.

than half a century ago, has created a widely known regimental image. The support services, with specific tasks to be carried out, have in their ranks more specialists who draw higher pay than foot soldiers of equivalent rank, and as a rule offer very much better promotion prospects together with opportunities for learning a 'trade'; and these factors undoubtedly help, if in a rather different way, the sense of *esprit de corps*. Of the Royal Army Medical Corps it must be said that it has a remarkable record of awards to its members for gallantry under fire. One medical officer, Captain N. G. Chavasse, won the Victoria Cross on two separate occasions.

The problem of attracting recruits to a volunteer army is, as we have seen, a continuing one. Once in the ranks, the new soldier is taught to have a sense of pride in himself and in his regiment or corps. The Brigade of Guards does this superbly well, but so too do others. The cry of the drill sergeant to a squad of recruits being taught to march on the barrack Square, 'Swing those arms . . . Bags of swank . . . ', are re-echoed in training depots throughout the army, as they have been for a long, long time. If pomp and discipline emerge as the army's way of training its soldiers, including its tradesmen, specialists and technicians, it seems not unreasonable to ask how this works in practice in the daily life of other ranks. The answer is that it works surprisingly well. The army is a life apart, and the gap between soldiers and civilians is extremely wide. For the period of the two world wars, of course, this generalisation needs to be modified, because a great national army is by no means a small regular army writ large. Regular soldiers live in a small world. They can laugh at themselves and members of other units, they can mock their own traditions, precisely because they are secure in their membership of a community different from the 'civvies' of society at large. Fragments of such attitudes in the past are to be found in the nicknames which regiments and corps were given, or sometimes gave themselves – and there is no reason to suspect that they have greatly changed in the contemporary army, although they are more difficult to identify.

The Royal Army Service Corps, for example, was given its 'Royal' prefix in 1918 in commemoration of its work in the Great War. Since 1965 it has been redesignated the Royal Corps of Transport. In a previous incarnation it was known as the Land Transport Corps, and many troops in the Crimea referred to it as the 'London Thieving Company'. Later, as the Army Service Corps, it was sometimes called 'Ally Sloper's Cavalry' after a comic character popular from the 1880s to the early 1920s. The Life Guards were once nicknamed 'The Piccadilly Butchers' after they had charged a mob during a political riot in 1804. The 7th Dragoon Guards, now incorporated in the 4th/7th Royal Dragoon Guards, spent a long period in Ireland during the early eighteenth century, and a nickname still recorded, 'The Virgin Mary's Bodyguard', recalls this period during which they recruited many Roman Catholics into their ranks. The best nickname of all is certainly 'Tommy Atkins', the generic name for the individual soldier. It dates from August 1815, when individual record-of-service books were first given to each man in the ranks. The specimen form sent

Private George Bryant, champion shot of the British army in 1873. His pipeclayed equipment, including rifle sling, bears witness to much hard work. His regiment, the 62nd, illustrates the complexities of military tradition over more than two centuries. Four regiments have had this number: the first was raised in 1743, named Battereau's after its colonel; the next in 1755, The Royal Americans; the third in 1756, 1st Highland Battalion. Bryant belonged to the regiment which was raised in 1758 and which, through amalgamation and change of name, is known in today's army as The Duke of Edinburgh's Royal Regiment.

out with the book showed how details should be filled in, and at the place where a signature was required, there was the hypothetical name 'Thomas Atkins' (or for illiterate men, 'Thomas Atkins×his mark'). The term 'Tommy' was later popularised by Rudyard Kipling.

Acronyms and decorations readily lent themselves to mockery. At the end of the Second World War in Europe an organisation known as Allied Military Government of Occupied Territory was set up. Many senior and elderly officers were concerned in AMGOT, which soon became known as 'Ancient Military Gentlemen on Tour'. Hardly fair, perhaps . . . at any rate, the name was soon changed. Even more astringent has been the reaction of men in the ranks to the honours awarded to high-ranking officers. The CMG, for instance, was cynically interpreted as a command: 'Call me God'. Holders of the KCMG were less peremptory: 'Kindly call me God'. Irreverent attitudes made explicit by such phrases do much to prevent pomp and circumstance from being taken too seriously. A little healthy and robustly expressed cynicism is no bad thing. The great soldiers of art and fiction, 'Old Bill' and 'The Good Soldier Švejk', rather than a real life Wellington or Napoleon, set the tone for such attitudes. Paradoxically it is mild iconoclasm which ensures the survival of tradition, and indeed holds the army together.

Going for a soldier today is remarkably similar to what it was when Sergeant Kite was beating up for recruits in Shrewsbury, or when Private Edge was plodding up to his comrades in the front line on the Somme with cigarettes. The technologies have changed; but, as anyone who has ever 'gone for a soldier' will probably admit, the personnel have not.

Hanging about: a good deal of time in the army has always been spent in simply waiting around, feeling bored . . . These men are awaiting embarkation for South Africa at the turn of the century.

FURTHER READING

There are references to studies and memoirs throughout the text, but in addition I have selected from a potentially vast bibliography books that have bearing on other ranks in particular. Discussion of how other ranks in the British Army have been recruited, and how they have lived, is patchy. The best books to touch on the subject in anything more than a superficial manner cover the period up to 1814. Among them are J. Childs, *The British Army of William III*, 1987; C. Duffy, *The Military Experience in the Age of Reason*, 1987; C.H. Firth, *Cromwell's Army*, 1902, 3rd edition 1921; S.R. Frey, *The British Soldier in America*, 1981; Sir C. Oman, *Wellington's Army 1809–1814*, 1913, 1986; A. Brett-James *Life in Wellington's Army*, 1972; J. Prebble, *Culloden*, 1961 and reprints; R.E. Scouller, *The Armies of Queen Anne*, 1966. John Keegan, *The Face of Battle*, 1976 and reprints, discusses five battles from Agincourt to the Somme.

For later periods there are many lacunae. E.M. Speirs, *The Army and Society 1815–1914*, 1980, is useful. The army which went to war in South Africa is well, if tersely, described in J.M. Grierson, *Scarlet into Khaki*, 1899, 1988. Fortunately, however, memoirs written by serving soldiers began to appear in the late eighteenth century, and from the period of the Peninsula War onwards they were published in modest profusion. There is a good selection of them in Roy Palmer, *The Rambling Soldier*, 1977, which also contains an extensive bibliography. See also C. Field, *Echoes of Old Wars*, 1934; T.H. McGuffie, *Rank and File*, 1964.

For 1914 to 1918 C.B. Purdom, *Everyman at War*, 1930, which contains sixty personal narratives, has stood the test of time, but has not, I think, been reprinted. There are numberless books about experiences in the Second World War, but there is nothing like Purdom's anthology. E. Shephard, *A Sergeant-Major's War*, 1987, is one of the very few accounts of active service by other ranks. Trevor Royle, *The Best Years of their Lives*, 1986, traces the lives of men conscripted between 1945 and 1963 largely in their own words. For today's army Tony Parker, *Soldier Soldier*, 1985, is recommended.

On more specialised themes coverage is equally uncertain. J. Fortescue, *A Short Account of Canteens in the British Army*, 1928, and H. Miller, *Service to the Services. The Story of Naafi*, 1971, are wide ranging and authoritative. V. Bamfield, *On the Strength. The Story of the British Army Wife*, 1974, is brief but full of good things. J. Thompson, *The Other Army. Camp Followers of the English Civil War*, n.d., Partizan Press 1986, is both unusual and informative. An important book is K. Ballhatchet, *Race, Sex and Class Under the Raj*, 1980, devoting several chapters to the sexual problems of the army in Victorian India and discussing attempts to solve them. Harry Hopkins, *The Strange Death of Private White*, 1977, is about the flogging of a soldier in the 1840s and its consequences in terms of the way in which soldiers were regarded by their superior officers. The background detail is excellent.

Books apart, the illustrated quarterly *Journal of the Society for Army Historical Research* is a mine of information on a wide range of topics, particularly with regard to the social history of the army. Amongst many outstanding articles published in its pages there are two by R.L. Blanco which deal with original and contentious themes: 'The Attempted Control of Venereal Disease in the Army of Mid-Victorian England' (Vol. XLV No. 184, Winter 1967); and 'Attempts to Abolish Branding and Flogging in the Army of Victorian England before 1881' (Vol. XLVI No. 187, Autumn 1968). See also G. Tylden, 'The Accoutrements of the British Infantryman, 1640 to 1940' (Vol. XLVII No. 189, Spring 1969); M. Barthorp, 'Anatomy of a Troop and Squadron 10th Royal Hussars 1859–1872' (Vol. LXII No. 252, Winter 1984); C. T. Atkinson, 'Journal of William Todd' (Vol. XXIV Nos. 119 & 120, Autumn, Winter, 1951).

ACKNOWLEDGMENTS

The Albion Press Ltd would like to thank the following organisations for supplying illustrations and permitting their reproduction:
Arms & Armour Press 153
The Border Regiment and King's Own Royal Border Regiment Museum, Carlisle 25
BBC Hulton Picture Library 14, 34, 46, 55, 64, 76, 77, 83, 109, 124, 156
Imperial War Museum, London 12, 114, 115, 122, 135, 136
Mansell Collection 11, 15, 41, 42, 45, 59, 60, 86, 87, 88, 89, 99, 154
Mary Evans Picture Library 21, 24, 43, 111
Navy, Army & Air Force Institutes 69
Courtesy of the Director, National Army Museum, London 6, 9, 17, 28-29, 32, 35, 39, 48–9, 51, 68, 75, 78, 93, 94, 97, 138, 141, 150 (Courtesy of Regimental Museum of the Gloucestershire Regiment)
Scolar Press 3
Soldier Magazine 37
All other pictures are from private collections. The Albion Press would also like to thank the staff of the above organisations, and other Regimental and Army Museums, for their help in suggesting and locating suitable illustrations, and to thank Anne-Marie Erlich of ET Archive for her similar assistance.

Amongst the many debts incurred in the writing of this book, those that I acknowledge with the greatest pleasure are to Patrick Breen of NAAFI; Stanley Brett; Bill Fishman; R. Hoar of Beefeater Steak Houses; Joy Moody; Brian Robertson.

To Michael Cane, Hon. Editor of the *Journal of the Society for Army Historical Research,* an especial thank you. Over the years both he and his predecessors have provided a forum for all the contributors who have often, albeit unknowingly, set me on the right track.

Barbara Gilbert, as ever, was a tower of strength, not only typing the MS but reading the draft with the sharp and practised eye of a sergeant major.

Without Anne, my wife, the book could never have been written. Thank you . . . again.

VN

INDEX